AF647611

RURAL INDUSTRIAL MANAGEMENT

About the Author

Dr. N. Meenakshisundaram (*b.*1951), Ph.D. is working as Professor of Rural Industries and Management, Department of Rural Industries and Management, Gandhigram Rural Institute, Gandhigram, Dindigul District, Tamil Nadu. He has done his Ph.D. (1994) on "Khadi and Village Industries in Tamil Nadu – A Study of Financial Performance" from the Faculty of Commerce, Sri Krishnadevaraya University, Anantapur, Andhra Pradesh. He is a first rank holder and Gold medallist in his Post-Graduate Diploma in Rural Sociology and Community Development – M.C.D. (1975) from Gandhigram Rural Institute, Gandhigram. M.A.(Sociology) (1979) Mysore, M.Com. (1981) (S.V. University).

Dr. N. Meenakshisundaram is an experienced faculty member in Rural Industries and Management and has been teaching Accounts, Financial Management, Costing, Principles of Management, Marketing Management, Marketing Research, Rural Industrialisation and Management of Medium and Small Enterprises for B.A., M.A. and M.Phil. students of Rural Industries and Management and a guide for Research scholars doing Ph.D. Programmes in Rural Industries and Management.

He has published more than 25 research articles related to entrepreneurship and management in Rural Industries in the national journals like Khadi Gramodyog, Social Welfare, Indian Management, The Business Intelligence, Journal of Extension and Research, The Co-operation etc., and has been associating himself with entrepreneurship development and management programmes conducted by National Small Industries Corporation (NSIC), Khadi and Village Industries Commission (KVIC), District Industries Centre (DIC), District Rural Development Agency (DRDA) and various universities. He has guided several Ph.D. scholars and offering consultancy services to small enterprises and also was author and co-author of 4 books.

RURAL INDUSTRIAL MANAGEMENT

Edited by

Dr. N. Meenakshisundaram

M.C.D., M.A., M.Com., Ph.D.
Professor & Head
Department of Rural Industries and Management,
Gandhigram Rural Institute, Deemed University,
Gandhigram- 624302, Dindigul (T.N), India

CONCEPT PUBLISHING COMPANY, NEW DELHI-110059

Cataloging in Publication Data—DK
Courtesy: D.K. Agencies (P) Ltd. <docinfo@dkagencies.com>

Rural industrial management / [edited by] N. Meenakshisundaram.
p. cm.
Contributed articles.
With special reference to India.
Includes bibliographical references.
Includes index.
ISBN 818069352X

1. Rural industries—India—Management. I. Meenakshisundaram, N. (Nallasivam), 1951-

DDC 338.095 4 22

All rights reserved. No part of this work may be reproduced, stored in a retrieval system or transmitted in any form or by any means, electronic, mechanical, photocopying, microfilming, recording or otherwise, without the prior written permission of the copyright owner and the publisher.

ISBN : 81-8069-352-X (HB)

First Published 2006

© N. Meenakshisundaram (*b.*1951)

Published and Printed by
Ashok Kumar Mittal
Concept Publishing Company
A/15-16, Commercial Block, Mohan Garden
New Delhi-110059 (India)

Phones : 25351460, 25351794
Fax : 091-11-25357103
Email : publishing@conceptpub.com

Foreword

Mahatma Gandhi had strong conviction that the economic problems of Rural India could be solved through establishment of Rural Industries. These industries have contributed to the development of Indian economy in the recent years. They are potential generators of employment, particularly in rural areas. These rural industries have added substantial income to the nation. And the rural industries are labour intensive and capital saving using simple local technologies. The products of rural industries developed a 'niche' in the marketing. Despite these strengths, the rural enterprises suffer in functional areas of management like financial management, human resource management, marketing management.

Therefore in this book micro level studies related to the functional areas of management and the policy support needed are explained. In this direction, the book edited by Dr. N. Meenakshisundaram, Professor of Rural Industries and Management, Gandhigram Rural Institute – Deemed University, Gandhigram, Tamil Nadu and published by Concept Publishing Co., New Delhi will be highly useful to the students and research scholars in Rural Industries and Management, Commerce, Management, Economics and Training Institutions in Rural Development, Rural Industries and KVIC.

Date : June 8, 2005

Dr. N. Thillainayagam
Professor & Head,
Department of Rural Industries
and Management,
Gandhigram Rural Institute,
Gandhigram.
Tamil Nadu

Foreword

Acknowledgements

I deeply express my thanks to Prof. Dr. T. Karunakaran, Vice-Chancellor, Gandhigram Rural Institute, Prof. Dr. M. Sundaravadivelu, Registrar, Gandhigram Rural Institute, Prof. Dr. G. Pankajam, Former Vice-Chancellor, Gandhigram Rural Institute, Prof. Dr. P. Kanniappan, former Registrar, Gandhigram Rural Institute, Dr. G. Palanidurai, Prof. and Head of Political Science & Development Administration and Dean, FRSS, Gandhigram Rural Institute and Dr. N. Thillainayagam, Prof. and Head, Department of Rural Industries and Management for having encouraged the book writing work with the title 'Rural Industrial Management'. I also express may gratitude to the faculty members who contributed papers on various aspects of Rural Industrial Management.

My colleagues for their valuable assistance deserve high appreciation. I thank Sri Senthil, Rural Industries and Management Department for computer typing.

I am thankful to Prof. M.S. Prabakaran, Department of English and Dr. R. Seerangarajan, Reader, Department of Rural Industries and Management, Gandhigram Rural Institute for having corrected the scripts.

Finally, I express my thanks to secretarial staff of the Department of Rural Industries and Management who have rendered innumerable services in completing the work successfully and to Concept Publishing Company, New Delhi for having brought out this book in a nice form.

N. Meenakshisundaram

Acknowledgements

[illegible]

Contents

List of Tables

List of Figure & Graphs

Figures

Graphs

1

Rural Industries :
Nature and Scope

N. MEENAKSHISUNDARAM

India has appreciably developed in the fields of industry, communication, agriculture, science and technology etc. especially during the post independent era. Inspite of such advancements, poverty is still prevalent in rural India due to unemployment and under employment. Our rural population is mainly depended on agriculture for their livelihood. Since agriculture is a seasonal occupation, people are unable to get employment and adequate earning for their food security. Hence, prevalence of poverty.

Poverty is perhaps as old as human society. The word poverty is derived from the Latin pauper which means 'scarce' or 'few'. It indicates that poverty is, broadly speaking, a state or condition of the person or the habitual state of being poor. Though the word poverty is used figuratively in the sense of spiritual well-being or its opposite, it relates primarily to the physical state of man. The three basic needs of man viz., food, clothing and shelter are said to be its great guide posts. The persons who lack the necessaries of life, who have the means but fail to apply them and who have no appreciable margin above wants are said to being poverty.

In order to minimise the prevalence of poverty, rural industries can play a vital role in providing rural employment resulting in food security to rural people.

Rural industries are those viable Village and Small Scale Industries that can be established in rural areas using rural technology, labour and capital. Establishment of such Village and Small Scale Industries would provide employment to local people, reduce migration of village people from rural to urban in search of employment, raise the standard of living of local people. Most of these industries are capital light and labour intensive.

Characteristics of Rural Industries:

Rural industries are called village industries, cottage industries, traditional industries and agro-industries. The characteristics of these industries can be stated as follows :

(1) Rural industries are highly decentralised. The producers are dispersed over a wide area.
(2) They are self employment enterprises — Owners, Managers, Labour — all combined.
(3) Simple technologies are employed.
(4) Family members are workers.
(5) No strict time schedule for work is followed. The members work according to their convenient time.
(6) The capital requirement is low-around Rs.1,00,000 per artisan.
(7) Gestation period is short.
(8) Raw materials available in rural areas are widely used.
(9) Products are produced mainly to meet local demand.
(10) Low energy consumption.
(11) Rural industries are mainly labour intensive.
(12) Generally hereditary, except in case of modern village industries.
(13) They are non-polluting and enviro-friendly.

Types of Rural Industries

The rural industries fulfilling the above characteristics are:

(1) Khadi and Village Industries (Soap, Bakery, Handmade Paper, Ghani Oil, Fruit Processing, Masala Powder Unit, etc.)
(2) Handlooms
(3) Sericulture
(4) Coir Industries
(5) Handicrafts

Khadi and Village Industries

Khadi and Village Industries are suitable to rural areas in providing employment opportunities at a very modest capital investment.

Khadi is defined as "cloth woven on handlooms from yarn spun by hand in India from cotton, wool, silk or a mixture of these fibres". This industry is very traditional and uses locally available cotton as raw material in villages. To Gandhiji, therefore, Khadi was a symbol of economic freedom and equality, and the charka became the symbol of Swadeshi movement.

Village Industries

Now village industry means any industry located in a rural (areas) population of which does not exceed 20,000 or such other figure which produces any goods or renders any services with or without use of power and in which fixed capital investment (in plant and machinery and land and building) per head of an artisan does not exceed one takh rupees.

Employment in Rural Industries

The number of persons employed in rural industries is as follows:

Table 1.1 : Persons Employed in Rural Industries

Sector	*Persons In lakh*
1. Khadi	14.71
2. Village Industries	28.89
3. Handloom	78.19
4. Sericulture	60.30
5. Handicrafts	38.30
6. Coir	3.10
Total	223.49

Those who are employed in rural industries especially in Khadi and Village Industries can earn from Rs.30 to Rs.75 per day. In order to improve the earning capacity of persons employed in rural industries a number of measures have been introduced in the field of technology and production process. And the employment potential of this sector depends upon its capacity to progress well.

Some of the micro level research studies on rural industries reveal the following :

Organisation

The Rural Industries programmes are run by individuals, guilds, institutions and co-operatives. It is found that a large number of artisan co-operatives engaged in village industries have continued to remain dormant because of poor management of affairs.

Marketing

The various national level boards have put up sales outlets in important cities and towns. And also assisting institutions to open their own sales centres for marketing of rural industrial products. It is found that such outlets are not adequate. The aggressive marketing approach such as consumer needs, price advertisement must be adopted to improve sales.

Training for Personnel

Training is one of the methods of improving the quality of human factor in industries and other sectors for effective contribution towards goal achievement of organisations. In rural industries the artisans are not having adequate formal education. Therefore, there is a need for training in large scale covering more number of artisans and other interested people in establishing rural industries.

There is a need for assessment of existing training programmes of KVIC, Coir, Handicrafts, Silk Industries etc. related to skill development in product manufacturing technology and in supervisory and management training courses. This would enable the training centres to redesign their programme if necessary.

Finance

Finance or capital is very essential for any organisation. The rural industries are no exception. The financial requirements can conveniently be classified into capital expenditure and working capital. The former is meant for the acquisition of fixed assets such as land, building, machineries furniture and fittings etc. and the latter is for the purchase of raw materials, payment of services. Most of the entrepreneurs and institutions do not have adequate capital. And it is difficult to mobilise funds from institutional agencies as they are unable to fulfil the requirements for getting loan such as security, profitability position etc. Therefore, there is a need for suitable financial supporting schemes that would enable the rural industrial entrepreneurs to get finance from institutional financing agencies.

Raw Materials

The products produced in rural industries are also produced in medium and large scale industries. Production of edible oils, Neo soap, Footwear, Bakery products, Vegetable and Fruit preservation are some of the examples. The prices of these raw materials are frequently fluctuating as they are products of agriculture. Hence, the entrepreneurs could not make seasonal procurement of such raw materials and supply at cheaper price. Through establishment of raw material bank, this would make the products more competitive.

The rural industries can contribute to the national economy significantly. For this purpose there is a need for proper planning and more participation on the part of the Government, NGOs and Universities in promoting rural industries and upgrading their products which would result in higher employment opportunities in rural areas and porerty eradication.

REFERENCES

1. Sivayya K.V., Indian Industrial Economy, S.Chand & Co., 1990.
2. Vasand Desai, Organisation and Management of Small Scale Industries, Himachal Publications, 1995.
3. Jhingan M.L. The Economics of Development and Planning, Konark, 1995.
4. Publications of Khadi and Village Industries Commission, Mumbai.

2

Export Management of Handloom Products

N. MEENAKSHISUNDARAM

Rural Industries play an important role in the development and diversification of rural economy. The rural industries are of many types such as Khadi and Village Industries, Handloom, Coir, Sericulture and Handicrafts etc. And these industries are labour intensive and capital saving that are well suitable for developing countries. The products of these industries can be used in our daily life. Of these industries, the share of handloom industry in the process of rural industrialisation is very significant and the handloom products are marketed within India and in foreign countries.

The Handloom Industry in India has a very long history spanning over several centuries. Textile production in this country commenced with handlooms and the passage of time has not lessened the role of the industry completely. The industry continues as a partner with decentralised powerloom sector, mill sector and the khadi sector. As a traditional industry, handloom has been serving the basic needs of the people.

It may hereby pointed out that the handloom industry has a great potential for the utilisation of human resources. It is necessarily a labour-intensive industry. In a country with considerable unemployed man power and increasing rate of unemployment then any investment that can utilise idle human resources is welcome. For this reason the handloom industry has a great role to play in the economic development in future. This being the fact, it is possible that with less capital and more labour, a productive system can be maintained for the manufacture of the quality goods. With growing rural unemployment, the time has come to utilise our labour resources both in urban and rural through development of handlooms. The handloom industry and exports provide a great opportunity for such utilisation. Indian exports made phenomenal growth from 4.9 per cent growth in 1980-85 to 18.2 per cent growth in 1985-90s. In 1990-95 India has recorded 12.8 per cent annual growth of which major growth occurred after the introduction of liberalisation policies.

Among the Indian total exports, low technology production constitute major share at about 52 per cent during 1996s. Low Technology products are textiles, Leather products-footwear, furniture and simple plastic products. Hence, these products tend to have less capital intensive and simple technologies, low R & D expenditures, skill requirements and low scale of economies. These products have low entry barriers and preferred for its low price rather than its quality or technology.

Table 2.1 : Trends in Exports of Textiles

(Value in Thousands of US $)

S.No.	*Item*	*1980*	*1990*	*Annual Percent age growth*	*1995*	*Percent- age growth*
1.	Textile Exports	1430877	3347110	13.31%	6931610	10.7%
2.	Total Exports	4527906	13195949	19.1%	23929986	8.1%
3.	Percentage of textiles export to total export	32%	26%		29%	

From Table 2.1, one can understand that around 30 per cent of textiles of total exports contribute to India's major export earnings. These items are in market niches (such as ethnic garments) that have the risk of saturation at anytime. Further, growth in exports of textiles from 1980 to 1990s and 1990s to 1995s were recorded @ 13.39 per cent per annum and @ 21.7 per cent per annum respectively. The above rates of growth in low technology areas are higher when compared to world growth rate of 5.7 per cent per annum. In Indian context, these decentralised textile exports have a big role to play in the years to come. These traditional textiles are labour intensive and support in promoting rural employment as these items are mainly produced in rural areas and suburban areas.

The handloom products are exported to countries such as Malaysia, Singapore, USA, Dubai, Hong Kong, Korea etc., contributing to the export earnings of India.

A study was undertaken during the year 1999 on export

management of Handloom fabrics and made ups with a view to study the potentiality of exports, growth rate of various products exported and to suggest solutions for their better performance. The study covered a period of 5 years from 1993 to 1998.

Export Management of Handloom Fabrics and Made-Ups

The goods produced and their outflow from a country is known as export. It is for economic growth and many economic development indicators are based on export earnings of a country. Under the globalisation era, exporting is considered as one of the key activities for prosperity. It ensures a nation greater stability and growth. It also widens the market for national products which, *inter alia*, enables them to obtain a better price for their products. It also gives more employment. The countries which have more than producing they require for their own use are, therefore, able to sell their surplus and deficient in them and are willing to buy.

Export Management

The major functions of export management is to ensure higher degree of efficiency during the course of investigating markets, creating demands for the product and maintaining sales in the overseas market. Export executive in an organisation get the things done through group efforts.

Export of Handloom Goods

The handloom exports are divided into two categories. They are :

(1) Fabrics (Non-made-ups)
(2) Made ups.

Fabrics

1. Real Madras Handkerchiefs
2. Lungies
3. Dhoties/Sarees
4. Shirtings
5. Other fabrics

Made-Ups

Table cloth, seating mats, napkins, kitchen towels, tea towels, bed spread, bed sheet, dish cloth, bed cover, bags, cushion covers, kitchen co-ordinates, floor swaps, pillow covers, terry towels, thorthu towels and furnishing cloth.

Analysis of Data

The present study has been attempted to assess the growth and trend analysis of various handloom items and products with linear equation in the form y = c + mx where 'm' indicates the growth rate or trend of a particular item.

The analytical frame work gives a suitable direction to guide the export unit and what to export, how much to export and when to export and where to export on the basis of mathematical models to analyse the trend position and give future steps to improve exports.

In respect of handloom fabrics, the 'm' value has been calculated and presented in Table 2.2

Table 2.2 : Growth Rate of Quantity and Value

S. No.	*Items*	*Growth rate of quantity (MQ)*	*Growth rate of value (mv)*
1.	RMHK	3.46	68.9
2.	Lungies/Sarongs	–11.49	–4.49
3.	Dhoties & Sarees	–0.13	–3.56
4.	Shirtings	–2.42	–60.51
5.	Others	3.39	–29.57
	Average	0.6689	5.984

It presents the growth rate and trend value for quantity (mQ) of an item exported and value (mv) of the respective exports.

Invariably all the items of exports except RMHK fabrics have recorded negative values in growth indicating a backward trend for the handloom fabrics. In general handloom fabrics have limited scope for exports as value added items has found increased usage.

Negative growth rates in respect of lungies, sarongs, dhoties and sarees may be attributed to the following reasons :

(a) Major market in South East Asian countries and the

recessionary trends in those countries Malaysia, Singapore etc., affected the export performance of lungies, sarees and dhoties.

(b) Severe competition developed by China, South Korea, Taiwan and Pakistan for Indian Handloom fabrics in the markets of Japan and Arabian countries.

(c) Japan imports floor coverings, that has been occupied by Chinese products of cheaper price due to possible reduction in freight charges from China to Japan.

The above trends coupled with lack of Government support mechanism has led to fall in exports of handloom fabrics.

Table 2.3 : Made-Ups

S. No.	*Items*	*Growth rate of quantity*	*Growth rate of value*
1.	Floor coverings	–0.55	–178.22
2.	Bed covers/Bed spreads	–0.01	–37.03
3.	Pillow covers & table cloths	0.31	21.63
4.	Towels & Napkins	0.19	45.48
5.	Others	–5.11	–800.99
	Average	–1.034	–208.02

Table 2.3 indicates the growth rate of handloom made-ups for each items. Floor coverings recorded growth rate (-) 0.55 in terms of quality exports and -178.22 in terms of value of exports. This negative rate value is an indication of declining trend in terms of Floor covering which are catered by Chinese and Pakistani exports. To meet the competition, export promotional measures by Government and export units should be undertaken. In terms of bed linen, it has recorded negative growth rates in quantity of exports as well as value of exports. Product diversification will be right strategy to boost exoprts such as exploring new uses of the existing products and enhancing the value of the product through appropriate ornamentation of bed linens using cross-border jacquards. Table linens and pillow covers which are personal products and furnishing materials have shown positive growth rate 0.31 for quantity and 21.3 for value. This is the area where further concentration and specialisation are needed to further develop in to better prospects.

Towels have recorded positive growth rate signalling a revival for towelling materials and to improve the exports through quality control and use of azo free dyes and timely delivery schedule may be adopted. Other made-ups, like Aprons, Napkins, furnishing material which have shown positive growth rate for both quantity and values. In handloom made-ups design coupled with assessment of consumer preference, ethnic will improve the export performance. If the quota system be removed by importing countries, it will be a great problem for Indian handloom exports. And in order to tide over the critical position in 2003. It is necessary to strengthen and stabilize the handloom exports by adopting the measures suggested.

Handloom products have been exported in tune with the target. However, the prices of handloom products are higher, when compared with the products of China, Pakistan etc. The quality must also improve, price must be cheaper, strict and time bound schedule of delivery of goods are to be ensured for better performance in future. And, thus, the labour intensive handloom industry may generate more employment opportunities in our country.

Conclusion

Handloom industry operate in an environment of competition and subsidy. In this context handloom exports made significant progress for its ethnicity, intricate designs and delicacy. For the sustenance of handloom exports and to meet the international standards, the handloom exporting units should undertake standardisation, quality control of the products and reducing the cost of manufacture of the handloom goods through improving the efficiency of operations. To ensure quality of handloom products the weavers and other staff engaged in production activities may be given training on quality management. In this regard, national and state level handloom promotional organisations can arrange for appropriate quality management training programmes to the handloom exporters.

The above measures are indicative to improve handloom exports and the future prospects could be ensured if appropriate revival strategies are adopted. Such strategies will also help in the export earnings of Indian in the years to come.

REFERENCES

1. Aluvaliah and Little, *Economics of Development*, Oxford Publishing House, London 1996. pp. 241-243.
2. *HEPC News & Letter* - HEPC, Chennai, Vol.XXXI No.12, 1998.
3. *Handloom Export* - HEPC, Chennai - April 97 - March 98, Oct 1998.
4. *Handloom Export* - 1997-98 HEPC, Chennai 1996-97 April 1998 HEPC, Chennai, September '97.

3

Manufacturing Policy for Rural Industries

N. THILLAINAYAGAM

Manufacturing Sector in India

India is having a population of 1027 millions, of which 493 million are men and 534 million are women. Among the total population 368 million are in the workforce, 277 million are unemployed, 382 million are non-employed population. The employed persons are engaged in agriculture, industry and services; i.e., in the organised sector 25.76 million, in the unorganised sector 342.24 million. The unemployment in India is caused due to non-possession of required resources and non-possession of required skills. Out of the total population, 102.7 million are educated upto Higher Secondary stage and they have registered in employment exchanges, but they were not offered with jobs for want of positions. 174.3 million are less educated and they have not registered with employment exchanges; but they also need jobs. Totally, it is the manufacturing, business and service sectors which will have to provide employment to 277 million persons. The workforce in India is constituted with 36 per cent of the total population; agriculture 60 per cent, industry 16 per cent, services 24 per cent. The unemployment causes poverty, less income and less purchasing power with the people. The unemployment in India is the greatest problem, inspite of its rich resources. Every policy in India is to be examined and shaped only in the context of its problems. Manufacturing sector policy is the key policy for solving the problems of India.

Indian manufacturing is concerned mainly with food products, textile goods, cosmetics, wearing materials, household goods, furniture and building materials. These goods are produced in a large scale, medium and small scale industries. In the manufacturing sector, there are highly educated employees, skilled workers and unskilled, uneducated daily wage earners. Any policy in India is only for its people. And hence, the manufacturing policy of India cannot ignore the people of India. All along in the last Nine Five Year plans, the manufacturing policy of the Nation has ignored its people, therefore, India's economic problems could not be solved and they remain so strongly. In the Tenth Plan also under the compulsion of the World Trade Agreement, if the manufacturing policy is only for production of world trade-oriented goods, India will again become under colonial administration of the western countries.

Today, India's problem is not the production of goods or promotion of world trade, but eradication of poverty, unemployment and lower productivity. World Trade will bring only huge factories for manufacturing, higher level technology in use of machines, mass production of goods and whole sale international business houses. These achievements will not solve the problem of poverty and unemployment, rather it will only increase the poverty and unemployment. When foreign goods freely come in at cheaper rates, Indian goods cannot compete with them and hence the home production will go down correspondingly. If home production goes down, employment will be lost, income will be lost and the poverty will increase. Therefore, careful attention is to be made while framing the manufacturing policy in India. India has not developed itself to the stage of facing world competition. The industries are not competent enough to maintain the qualities of world standard. There are several measures to be attended for raising the standard of industries. Skill development to the workers to meet out the new requirement is one of them. In every industrial unit there are skilled workers and unskilled workers. Research studies indicate that 61 percentage of workers are unskilled in tiny sector, 25 per cent in Small Scale Industries, 25 per cent in Khadi and Village Industries, and 72 per cent are skilled in the manufacturing sector including 59 per cent in tiny sector, 60 per cent in Small Scale Industries, 68 per cent in Khadi and Village Industries, 82 per cent in Industrial Co-operatives. There is a need to make the unskilled workers into skilled workers. Strategies are to be evolved to make them skilled through proper training programmes. Without the effort the problem of quality in manufacturing sector cannot be solved. The quality of products and saleability of the products are the main concern for the manufacturing industries. Manpower should be suitably linked with manufacturing. Quality of the products and the quality of the man-power involved are the critical issues to the manufacturers. Under the World Trade Agreement, there is a threat of extinction to small scale manufacturing industries. The Small and Cottage level manufacturing sector are under threat now owing to the policy of globalisation. Globalisation aims at a free hand world market. There are advanced economies who are highly competent for a world market. Advanced technological inventions have facilitated technologically advanced countries in improving the quality of production; which has not happened in India. More than eighty per cent of the units in Indian manufacturing sector are traditional units with traditional technology. They need improvement. Still there is a long way to go in technological progress.

Government Policy for KVI

The Khadi and Village Industries are organised with a social objective of providing employment and with an economic objective of producing salable articles to meet out the local demands. The main objectives are promoting Khadi and Village Industries to create self reliance among the people, and to build up a strong Swadeshi spirit.

Government Policy for SSI Sector

The Small Scale Industrial Sector is to be viewed in terms of its volume of production, higher rate of employment and export potentiality. Therefore, the Govt. would have to urge deregulation of impediments, debureaucratisation, cluster approach in location, reservations of products, suitable trade policy for WTO compatibility, export promotion facilities, incentives for competitiveness, technology upgradation, improving the credit flow, revival of sick units, promoting the role of associations etc. The policy statement of Govt. of India 1991 makes special emphasis on access to institutional credit, removing bottle necks in marketing, compliance with cumbersome procedures, attending to technological observations intimating rearrangement by inspecting functionaries, removing labour laws, giving more operational flexibility adopting cluster approach in locating Small Scale Industries in specific industrial belts, upgradation of technologies, upgradation of capacity utilisation, enhancing supporting infrastructure, developing network of banking, strengthening the personnel, building up additional common warehousing facilities and so on. The policy statement also makes special emphasis on special industries such as electronics, textiles, automobiles and defence related industries.

Programmes for KVI during Ninth Plan Period

- The Khadi and Village Industries sector would have created 2 million new jobs during the remaining years of the Ninth Five Year Plan.
- The target of covering 50 districts under the special employment programme creating 10,000 jobs in each district would have been accomplished.
- To cover 125 blocks for development of Khadi and Village Industries providing employment to atleast 1,000 persons per block.
- The production of Khadi should be increased from the present level of 105 million sq. metres to 200 million sq. metres by the terminal year of the present plan and thus gradually two third to the cloth production by introduction of electricity in charkha operation and in loom operation.
- Development of Khadi should be given top priority by Khadi and Village Industries Commission.
- Extension of Khadi programme in the future should be primarily through special employment programme in selected backward districts.
- Rebate may be replaced by Market Development Assistance.
- Raw material banks may be opened near the production centres.
- Production of best quality Khadi for export should be taken up by selected institutions and they should be free to fix their own prices.
- The certification system should continue.
- The existing definition of village industry may be modified to raise the per capita investment limit in plant and machinery from the existing level of Rs.50,000 to economically viable level.
- During the remaining period of the Ninth Plan and the Tenth Plan period twenty million additional jobs should be created in village industries sector.
- The funding pattern approach has to be gradually changed and Khadi and Village Industries Commission/State Khadi and

Village Industries Board should adopt project approach on viability basis.

- KVIC and KVIBs have to concentrate their attention on a few selected industries for which they have developed necessary expertise and infrastructure.
- KVIC should give proper attention for development and transfer of appropriate technology.

Cluster Development Programme

There are nearly 2,500 artisan clusters in India. Most of these clusters consist of more than 100 artisans engaged in one or similar trade or activity. These artisans have inherited necessary technical skill from their ancestors. Thus they possess the strength of their in-born expertise and skill in their respective arts and crafts. Though most of them are not highly educated, they are masters of their own crafts. With the onset of industrial revolution and setting up of big industries based on modern technology, the tradition based tiny sector of artisans is essential that the traditional based tiny sector of artisans is struggling for its survival. Therefore, it is essential that the traditional clusters are strengthened after conducting a study of their present status, technology, input needs and other requirements.

India has over 200 vibrant clusters spread in different parts of the country. Some of them are located at Batala, Ludhiana, Surat, Indore, Kolhapur, Belgaum, Tirupur, Agra, Kanpur, Coimbatore, Firozabad, Aligarh, Mizapur, Bhadohi, etc. producing Leather-goods, Agricultural equipments, Textile, Hosiery, Textile Machinery, Carpet, Glass bangles, etc. Most of these clusters have been set up through a normal evolutionary process. Of late clusters of modern industries and hi-tech have also come up in Andhra Pradesh, Karnataka and Maharashtra. The Government tried to set up industrial township in various parts of the country which is also an attempt to develop industrial clusters though these multi-industrial clusters of heterogeneous activity.

The KVIC has been looking forward to promote and develop clusters of artisans by utilising their skills and expertise in rural areas of the country. The purpose of promoting these clusters is to enhance the level of earnings and sustainability of artisans and also to make them contribute sufficiently to the growth of national economy in right proportion to their strength and potential.

The KVIC initiated efforts for promoting artisan clusters in 1980s and early 90s but much could not be done. During last two years, these efforts have been revived and artisan clusters have come into greater focus with proper policy guidelines and input support for the same. The process of identification for the first phase has been completed and some of the clusters have started functioning. The KVIC had approved a list of 50 clusters wherein the programme would be launched during 1999-2000 itself. Another set of 50 clusters would be identified for the year 2000-2001. The programme has already been launched in the following clusters:

1. Angarha (Bihar) – Bee Keeping
2. Madurai (Tamil Nadu) – Non-edible Oil and Soap
3. Karnal (Haryana) – Leather
4. Saharanpur (U.P) – Bee Keeping

The programme is likely to be launched in remaining clusters. A booklet on "Development of Rural Industries". Clusters-Concept, Approach and Operating Guidelines was published and issued to all concerned for guidance and observance. Apart from this, workshops were conducted in all zones to have interaction with implementing agencies and field functionaries. It is expected that the Cluster Development Programme initiated by KVIC will pave the way for promotion of rural artisans in the country on a sound footing ensuring sustainability of their vocations and continuity of required inputs. The list of 50 clusters where the programme is being launched in the first phase is given below:

Common Facility Centre

1. Churu - Soap,
2. Sawai Madhopur – Handmade Paper
3. Hoshiarpur – Rural Engineering
4. Kullu – Bee keeping
5. Karnal – Leather
6. Surendra Nagar – Silk Khadi
7. Junagadh – Leather
8. Melghat – Cane and Bamboo
9. Jawahar – Fruit Processing Industries
10. Badlapur – Handmade paper
11. Kanpur Village – Soap
12. Varanasi Village – Fruit Processing and Bio-fertilizer
13. Sharanpur Village – Rural Engineering and Bee Keeping
14. Dehradun Village – Bee Keeping
15. Chitrakoot – MPI, FVPI, PCPI
16. Jaura – MPI, Bee Keeping
17. Bhagalpur Village – Oil
18. Muzaffarpur – Bee Keeping
19. Angarha – Bee Keeping

20. Pallitotalpada – Lime
21. Vhenjapura Village – REI
22. Jalpaiduri – Bee Keeping
23. Aizwal – Cane and Bamboo
24. Jirania – Cane and Bamboo
25. Itanagar – MPI/Bee Keeping
26. Khasi Hills – Bee Keeping
27. Silchar – Cane and Bamboo
28. Bijapur Village – Oil
29. Madurai Region – Soap
30. Madhavaram (Kadapakkam) – Palmgur
31. Calicut – Medicinal Plant Industries
32. Srikakulam – Ponduru Khadi
33. Narayanpur – Forest Based Industries
34. Chirai Dogri – MPI, FBI, Broom Making
35. Jashpurnagar – Bee Keeping
36. Dumka – Bamboo
37. Bishunpur – REI, PCPI, MPI
38. Palamu – Cane and Bamboo, FBI, Wool, Kambal Shawl
39. Hazaribagh – FIB, leaf cup
40. Chaibasa – Tassar
41. Lohardaga – REI, Utensil and Bee Keeping
42. Baliguda – Dungriguda – Bee Keeping, FBI, Leaf-cup
43. Robertsgunj – Medicinal Plant Industries
44. Raipur – Soap
45. Almora – Fruit and Vegetable Processing, MPI
46. Uttarkashi – Medicinal Plant Industries FVPI
47. Haldwani – Bee Keeping
48. Nangla, Chandrabhan – Leather and Village Oil
49. Dharwar – KVI
50. Arunachal Pradesh - Textiles

Note : MPI – Medicinal Plant Industries
FVPI – Fruits and Vegetable Processing Industries
REI – Rural Engineering Industries

On the basis of scheme circulated by the Ministry of Industry, Office of Development Commissioner, Small Scale Industries. Govt. of India, KVIC has decided to set up 50 Common Facility Centres per year in backward districts/rural areas to promote Village Industries in rural sector. The aim of the scheme is to provide various services besides backward and forward linkages and infrastructural facilities. The scheme has to be implemented through directly aided institutions of the KVIC.

Criteria for Selection of Common Facility Centre

(a) Before considering a proposal for establishment of Common Facility Centres, a comprehensive potential survey of the are a with reference to cluster units, concentration of artisans, availability of raw materials, marketability of the products etc. and also a techno-economic survey should be undertaken to ascertain genuineness and viability of the proposal.
(b) State Khadi and Village Industries Boards' own departmental

centres of their assisted institutions/co-operatives which have five years of experience in the related field, good tract record, sufficient land, building etc. to form as security for the fund, man power; and other desired infrastructure requirement will be given to the programme of Common Facility Centres.

(c) New NGOs which have five years experience in the related field, good tract record, sufficient land building etc. to form as security for the fund, man power and other desired infrastructure requirement along with the feasibility of the programme and desirability of investment will also be considered for Common Facility Centre Programme.

Financing Pattern

The maximum ceiling limit of funding for Common Facility Centres shall be upto Rs.2 crores and financing pattern will be as follows:

(1) 40 per cent from KVIC as grant (V.I. Plan)
(2) 45 per cent as loan from Consortium Bank Credit of the KVIC
(3) 15 per cent from directly aided institutions' contribution.

In addition to the above, the directly aided institutions should provide sufficient free hold land from their ownership.

Implementing Agencies

(i) A successful directly aided institution having a sound financial position.
(ii) The agency should extend services to satellite units of the district.
(iii) The period for setting up the project should not be more than 12 months.

Screening Committee

The Screening Committee has been formed to go into the details of proposal before it is placed for approval of Standing Finance Committee. The members of the Committee are as under :

1. Chairman, KVIC	:	Chairman
2. Chief Executive Officer, KVIC	:	Member
3. Dy. CEO (Village Industries)	:	Member
4. Head of the Dept. of Rural Technology III, New Delhi.	:	Member
5. Joint Chief Executive Officer, KVIC	:	Member/ Convenor

Release of Funds

Initially, loan and grant for building construction will be released. After ensuring proper utilisation of loan and grant, the funds for machinery/equipment will be released and working capital/revolving capital will be released after proper utilisation of funds released earlier.

Committee for Monitoring and Evaluation of the Project

1. Joint Executive Officer (Jt. CEO)	:	Chairman
2. Dy. CEO (Finance)	:	Member
3. Secretary of the implementing institution	:	Member
4. Two Representatives of facility users	:	Member
5. Directors of Specific Industries	:	Member
6. State/Regional Director	:	Member/ Convenor

Sarvodaya Brand

Need of Brand

(a) Branding is the activity which provides attribute and personality to a product and enhances its market.
(b) Brand name is used to make distinction of a particular product and influence the customer for developing the preference for its purchase.
(c) Brand creates a distinctive image of the product amongst the users.
(d) Brand makes a product an integrated product and offers many other attributes in addition to physical utility of the product.

Strength of KVI products :

(a) Eco-friendly,
(b) Bio-based and reliable,
(c) Natural,
(d) Excess Chemical-free and harmless,
(e) Helps generate employment,
(f) Exclusively with simple technology suited to rural homes.

Identification of Brand Name

The Khadi and Village Industries Sector serves as a lamp for the rural artisans lighting their homes and day-today life by providing employment and livelihood. The word 'Sarvodaya' means 'awakening for all' and hence is apt name to signify the activities and purpose of KVI sector and hence 'Sarvodaya' was rightly chosen as a brand name for Village Industries products.

Products Identified for 'Sarvodaya' Brand :

(a) Agarbathi,
(b) Honey,
(c) Pickles,
(d) Soap,
(e) Masala.

Modalities for 'Sarvodaya' Launch :

1. Departmental Bhavans will be nodal agencies for launching the Sarvodaya brand in the initial stage.
2. Identified institutions shall supply quality products identified under 'Sarvodaya' to the Departmental Bhavans.
3. Concerned Industry/Programme Directors will ensure online quality control as well as quality inspection before despatch of finished products.
4. Zonal Dy. C.E.Os will supervise to ensure that the 'Sarvodaya' brand is marketed through Sales Outlets of Khadi and Village Industries Institutions/Boards, Departmental Bhavans and Private Channels of distribution.

5. Package/labels designed by Indian Institute of Packaging and further developed by local professional agencies shall be supplied to the identified institutions on cost to cost basis.
6. Identified institutions shall also launch and market the Sarvodaya Brand through their existing sales outlets and will have to commit that within 6 months they will market all their identified products only under Sarvodaya Brand in the market.
7. Marketing consultancy shall be provided by M/s. Promotions and Premiums Consultants Private Limited, Mumbai (who has handled brands, Titan Watches, Ponds, Brook Bonds, Frooti, Tata Tea and Salt, Aristocrat Luggage, Whirlpool, Arvind Denim, etc.) has been selected for the brand launch and preparing marketing strategies.
8. A market survey had already been conducted through Centre for Bharatiya Marketing Development in the consumer markets of Mumbai, Delhi, Ernakulam and Bangalore to study the competitive prices etc. and based on their recommendation pricing policy has been formulated.
9. Institutions shall extend royalty of 1 per cent on the sales value to KVIC for the brand franchise offered to them which will meet a part of expenses towards marketing promotion etc.
10. Through initially Departmental Bhavans will co-ordinate and ensure procurement and supply of products under 'Sarvodaya' the objective will be to hand over the responsibility of marketing the 'Sarvodaya' brand to Federation/Consortium of identified institutions producing the Sarvodaya Brand products through various Khadi and Village Industries sales outlets as well as private sales channels of distribution. This shall be ensured in a phase wise manner within six months to one year. The role of Khadi and Village Industries Commission will be confined to providing inputs of marketing like advertisement, sales promotion, packaging, price fixation, etc.

Marketing Channel of Distribution

1. Initially the sales outlets of Khadi and Village Industries Commission, Khadi and Village Industries Boards and

institutions will be utilised for launching and marketing of 'Sarvodaya' brand products.

2. Simultaneously efforts will be made to launch and market products through private channels of distribution like wholesellers, retailers, Apna Bazar, Sahakari Bhandar, Gram Panchayat, etc.

Consortium Bank Credit

The Govt. of India has provided an amount of Rs.1,000 crores to the Khadi and Village Industries Commission through the Consortium of 15 nationalised banks, popularly known as Consortium Bank Credit for various Khadi and Village Industries Programmes. The amount will be available for viable and bankable projects under the Khadi and Village Industries sector on the guarantee of Central Government in respect of Khadi and Village Industries.

The Khadi and Village Industries Commission can on-lend the bank credit to the State/UT Khadi and Village Industries boards based on the guarantee of the respective State Govt. The Khadi and Village Industries Commission can also on lend the bank credits to its directly aided institutions, individual artisans and entrepreneurs.

Under Khadi and Polyvastra, the Consortium Bank Credit will not be available. Incase of Village Industries, capital expenditure loan and working capital loan would be covered under the Consortium Bank Credit. The Term Loan would be repayable in 28 quarterly instalments from 15th month onward. There would be a moratorium period of 12 months for repayment of principal as well as for payment of interest, which will be accumulated and paid in the 15th month along with interest is repayable in 7 years after moratorium period.

The rate of interest of Consortium Bank Credit for Village Industries would be average of prime lending rate (PLR) of 5 major members of the consortium, exclusive of interest tax. The interest would be calculated on quarterly basis.

The Khadi and Village Industries Commission would on-lend the Consortium Bank Credit to the State/UT Khadi and Village Industries Boards would levy 1 per cent as service charge.

The amount of Consortium Bank Credit is to be made available only after execution of the guarantee in favour of the Khadi and Village Industries Commission by the State Govt. concerned without which no funding will be done by the Khadi and Village Industries

Commission out of the CBC. The State/UT Khadi and Village Industries Boards would be fully responsible for recovery of Consortium Bank Credit borrowed by them from the Khadi and Village Industries Commission.

Margin Money Scheme

On the basis of recommendations for the High Power Committee report, submitted in May, 1994, headed by the then Prime Minister of India, the Khadi and Village Industries Commission launched a massive Rural Employment Generation Programme (REGP) on 2 October 1994 for generation of two million jobs under the Khadi and Village Industries Sector in the rural areas of the country.

In order to augment the Rural Employment Generation Programme, the Khadi and Village Industries Commission and Govt. of India introduced Margin Money Scheme with effect from 1st April 1995 for viable Village Industry Projects to be implemented in the rural areas defined under the Khadi and Village Industries Commission Act, 1956 amended upto date as under.

The area comprises any village and includes area comprised town, the population of which does not exceed 20,000 or such other figure as the Central Government may specify from time to time.

Any industry located in a rural area which produces goods or renders any service with or without the use of power and in which the fixed capital investment per head of an artisan or a worker does not exceed Rs.50,000 or such other sum as may be specified by Central Government from time to time.

Initially the Margin Money Scheme was implemented by linking it with Consortium Bank Credit (CBC) announced by the then Finance Minister while presenting the Union Budget for the year 1995-96 under which a line of credit of Rs.1000.00 crores was sanctioned in favour of the Khadi and Village Industries Commission for onward disbursement to its implementing agencies, State/U.T. Khadi and Village Industries Boards and institutions/societies registered with KVIC/KVIBs and rural entrepreneurs, craftsmen, artisans and individuals.

Since the rate of interest of CBC was related to the line of credit of Rs.1000.00 crores, the benefit of concessional interest was not available to the rural artisans, craftsmen, the small and rural entrepreneurs. Hence, in the second All India Conference of Industry

Ministry held on 11.02.1997 at Vigyan Bhavan, New Delhi, it was *inter alia*, announced that in order to minimise the burden of interest on village craftsmen, artisans and rural entrepreneurs, the Khadi and Village Industries Commission would deposit the Margin Money in advance with the Public Sector Banks who will be entrusted with the responsibility for implementing the Margin Money Scheme in the rural areas. Accordingly, after discussions with State Government functionaries and Bankers at various levels, a scheme for implementation of Margin Money Scheme through Scheduled Commercial (Public Sector) Banks was finalised in a meeting held at Reserve Bank of India on 22 July, 1997 which has since been circulated by Reserve Bank of India and Khadi and Village Industries Commission and the Head Offices of various Banks. The salient features of the Scheme are as under:

The scheme is applicable to all village industry projects set up in rural areas. The eligible agencies under the scheme are (i) individuals (rurak artisans/entrepreneurs) for projects upto Rs.10 lakhs and (ii) institutions, Co-operative Societies, trusts for projects upto Rs.25 lakhs.

25 per cent of the project cost upto Rs.10.00 lakhs will be provided by Khadi and Village Industries Commission as Margin Money by way of subsidy. For project above Rs.10.00 lakhs and upto Rs.25.00 lakhs, rate of Margin Money will be 25 per cent of Rs.10.00 lakhs plus 10 per cent remaining cost of the project.

In case of weaker section beneficiary viz. SC/ST/OBC/Women/ Physically Handicapped/Ex-servicemen and Minority Community beneficiary/institutions and for Hill, Border and Tribal Areas, North Eastern Region, Sikkim, Andaman & Nicobar Islands, Lakshadweep, Margin Money grant will be at rate of 30 per cent for the project cost upto Rs.10.00 lakhs and above this amount upto Rs.25 lakhs, it will be 10 per cent of the remaining cost of the project.

Under the scheme, the borrower is required to invest his own contribution of 10 per cent of the project cost. In case of SC/ST and other weaker section borrowers, the contribution will be 5 per cent of the project cost.

Banks will sanction 90 per cent of the project cost in case of general category borrowers and 95 per cent of the project cost in case of weaker section beneficiaries/institutions and disburse full amount of the loan.

Presently Khadi and Village Industries Commission is implementing Margin Money Scheme through Public Sector Banks, Regional Rural Banks and on selective basis through Co-operative Banks and Private Sector Scheduled Commercial Banks.

Programs for SSI

The programmes for SSI sector include cluster of SSI units, use of flexible manufacture system, inter firm co-operation, provision of service, collective agglomeration, research and development, common testing facility for qualities assurance, skill enhancement, information dissemination, entrepreneur competency development, networking of specialised agents in India and abroad, upgradation of technology, export and import facilities, subsidies for export, easy credit flow to small scale units, supply of scare raw material packages marketing intelligence, development of infrastructure of export units, participation in international exhibition, to promote marketing intelligence, facilitating the imports in other counters, re-orienting production and marketing strategies, promoting innovations alternatives audit by expert bodies, establishing research laboratories, venture capital scheme increasing working capital limits revival of sick units, establishing training institutes, evolving energy saving methods, formulating pollution control directions, online access to database and consultancy services, help line for SSI entrepreneurs, modernisation throw special schemes, enhancing capacity utilisation of SSI units and soon.

Production of Khadi and Village Industries

The production of Khadi from 1956-57 to 2002-03 in terms its monetary value are :

	Rs.
1956-57	8.23 crores
1989-90	257.88 crores
1996-97	626.40 crores
1997-98	624.10 crores
1998-99	635.90 crores
1999-2000	551.94 crores
2000-2001	431.57 crores
2001-2002	416.69 crores
2002-2003	443.07 crores

Production of Village Industries goods :

	Rs.
1956-57	12.73 crores
1989-90	1705.30 crores
1996-97	3885.85 crores
1997-98	3895.21 crores
1998-99	4476.48 crores
1999-2000	5613.41 crores
2000-2001	6491.69 crores
2001-2002	7140.52 crores
2002-2003	8126.30 crores

Production of Small Scale Industries Sector

Year	*No. of units in Lakhs*	*Output of current price Value in crores*
1994-95	25.71	Rs.
1995-96	27.24	3,56,213.00
1996-97	28.57	4,12,636.00
1997-98	30.14	4,65,171.00
1998-99	31.21	5,27,515.00
1999-2000	25.04	8,16,000.00
2000-2001	26.72	8,90,000.00

Employment in Khadi

S. No.	*Year*	*Person in lakhs*
1	1956-57	8.81
2	1989-90	14.12
3	1996-97	14.79
4	1997-98	14.01
5	1998-99	13.87
6	1999-2000	12.00
7	2000-2001	10.00
8	2001-2002	8.48
9	2002-2003	8.58

Employment in Village Industries

S. No.	*Year*	*Person in lakhs*
1	1956-57	6.77
2	1989-90	32.14

Contd.

S. No.	Year	Person in lakhs
3	1996-97	43.38
4	1997-98	42.49
5	1998-99	44.44
6	1999-2000	47.00
7	2000-2001	51.00
8	2001-2002	54.16
9	2002-2003	57.87

Employment in Small Scale Industries Sector

S. No.	Year	No. of SSI units in lakhs	Person employed in lakhs
1	1994-95	25.71	146.56
2	1995-96	27.24	152.61
3	1996-97	28.57	160.00
4	1997-98	30.14	167.20
5	1998-99	31.21	171.58
6	1999-2000	25.04	177.30
7	2000-2001	26.72	–

Sales in Khadi and Village Industries

S. No.	Year	Khadi	Village Industries
1	2001-2002	527.86 crores	8383.49 crores
2	2002-2003	577.63 crores	9615.71 crores

Earnings in Khadi and Village Industries

S. No.	Year	Khadi	Village Industries
1	2001-2002	215.98 crores	2653.60 crores
2	2002-2003	229.68 crores	3075.40 crores

Export Status for Small Scale Industries Sector at Current Prices in crores

S. No.	Year	Value of export in crores Rs.
1	1994-95	29,068
2	1995-96	36,470

Contd.

S. No.	Year	Value of export In crores Rs.
3	1996-97	39,249
4	1997-98	44,437
5	1998-99	49,481
6	1999-2000	53,975
7	2000-2001	54,200

Suggested Policy Frame Work for Small Scale Industries

Socio-economic Objectives of Small Scale Industries Sector

The social objectives of Small Scale Industries Sector is employment generation through income generating activities. The economic objectives of Small Scale Industries sector is resource utilisation in rural areas improving labour productivity in rural communities, technological improvement in Small Scale Industries Sector, thus providing enough employment and adequate income with Swadeshi spirit.

Training Needs for Small Scale Industries Sector

There are associations for all types of industries. These associations will have to arrange training programmes for specific skill promotion. The District Industries Centres may conduct training in entrepreneurship. In the case of advanced training at the state level and at the regional level the small Industries service institutes may organise training on specific skills and specified estates may be utilised for the purpose of training. The District industries Centres may develop laboratories for the training purpose. In case of costly equipments and lab facilities may have to arrange facilities and for such facilities to keep up with the time and advancement in specified activities. In case of training in the process of product making institutions like Gandhigram, T. Kallupatty, Wardha and such other reputed voluntary institutions and non-governmental organisations may be utilised for training. Such training institutions are to be enlisted and widely published. Each Panchayat Union/Samithi may identify Small Scale Industrial concerns who are willing to undertake training programme for rural youth who are to be promoted as self-employed new entrepreneurs.

Modernisation of Small Scale Industries Sector

Modernisations includes, suitably designed modern work sheds, advanced machinery, higher level training to the workers, storage facilities, communication network, transport facilities, marketing information network, higher productivity, higher rate of returns and so on. The Small Scale Industries especially in rural areas suffer from a lot of disadvantages owing to scattered locations, inadequate transport, less trained manpower, lack of communications, absence of market information, difficulties in storage facilities and so on. These bottlenecks are to be removed to save the Small Scale and Tiny Sector.

Technological Upgradation

In each industry, the machinery available in different capacities with cost may have to be widely advertised by the National Small Industries Corporation and the Small Industries Service Institutes. Technological conference for small industrialists and exhibitions with advanced technologies in each industry are to be organised in every district thro' District Industries Centre. The list of machinery in each industry must be available with the District Industries Centre for facilitating the small entrepreneurs. In the case of new technology training may be organised by the *SISI* to update the skills of the workers and supervisors.

Quality Improvement in Small Scale Industries sector

Quality testing laboratories are to be organised by the District Industries Centre in every district. The latest improvement in products are to be exhibited in the District Industries Centre to bring awareness to the entrepreneurs on new product and new quality of product. The small entrepreneurs are to be constantly in touch with the District Industries Centre.

Productivity in Small Scale Industries Sector

The productivity in each industry is to be asserted by periodical research. The SISI, NSIC and Technical consultancy organisations and research institutions are to attend this work. These institutions may sponsor research projects to the colleges and universities to carryout the research work. For testing the quality and productivity, the facilities available in colleges and universities may be fully utilised.

Employment Generation in Small Scale Industries Sector

At present the percentage of employment in large industries is only 3 per cent, Small Scale Industries Sector is 17 per cent and tiny sector is 80 per cent of the industrial labour force. The industrial labour force will have to improve to a minimum of 75 per cent of the total labour force. And the Small Scale Industries sector will have to attract more workers from the agricultural sector to relieve the congestion of labour force in agriculture.

The total labour force in India is 368 millions. Of which agriculture is engaging 60 per cent of the workers i.e. 220.80 millions. The remaining 40 per cent of the workers are engaged in business, construction, mining, transport, cottage and Small Scale Industries and other services. In cottage industries the total absorption of above force is only 47.12 millions. In Small Scale Industries, the absorption of labour force by 1998-99 is only 10.0 millions. Cottage and Small Scale Industries sector together engages about 57.12 millions workers. This 57 millions will have to be doubles in the next ten years and a minimum of 100 million workers are to be absorbed in the tiny and sc. In a long run a perspective plan of absorbing 200 million workers is to be thought of in non-agricultural sector. Then only the problem of unemployment can be solved.

Export of Small Scale Industries Sector

The export of Small Scale Industries Sector by 2000-01 is worth of Rs.54,200 crores which is about 34 per cent of the total export earnings. But it is viewed that there should be a sustained growth rate of 20 per cent to 25 per cent per annum in future. On 1993-94 the growth rate of Small Scale Industries sector was 31.4 per cent; on 1999-2000 it has come down to 20 per cent . An increasing trend can be maintained thro' special incentives to the export oriented units.

Service Units and their Importance

The service units provide opportunities for self employment in Small

Scale Industries Sector. India's problem lies with only unemployment of educated youths and the only way to solve the unemployment problem is to impart production skills to the rural youths. The voluntary institutions are to be encouraged to organise intensive training especially to rural women in diary, poultry, bee keeping, sericulture, processing of cereals and pulses bakery products, fruit preservation, basket making, cane works, glass fibre products, glass wares, agarbathis, papad making, readymade garments, printing and dyeing, preparation of herbal medicine, manufacture of confectioneries, soft drinks, rexine products, coir products, oil pressing, shampoo making, phenyle production, soaps and detergents, toys processing and packing of continents, preparation of malts, etc.

Incentives to Small Scale Industries Sector

1. Allotment of developed plots with entire cost as loan without margin money.
2. Allotment of sheds under higher purchase scheme.
3. Machinery with cent per cent loan.
4. Working capital loan 100 per cent with minimum rate of interest.
5. Free technical consultancy services.
6. Nominal cost for testing facilities.
7. Nominal cost for common facilities.
8. Special incentives for Backward areas.
9. Allotment of scare raw materials.
10. Minimum cost for storage facilities.
11. Special power tariff to Small Scale Industries.
12. Transport facilities by the District Industries Centre and NSIC in the case of interstate and international transports.
13. Linking of export facilities with minimum export duties.
14. Import of raw materials with minimum import duties.
15. Revival of sick units by providing adequate working capital.
16. Extension of time for repayment of loan.
17. Expert opinion on capacity utilisation of the plant.
18. Expert help to study the indicators of sickness and to suggest remedial measures.
19. Provision of collateral security loans to sick units.

Impact of Globalisation of Small Scale Industries Sector

There is an urgent need to strengthen the Small Scale Industries Sector to face the challenges of World Trade Organisation. World Trade Organisation system must restrict imports in the face of increased competition resulting from liberalisation measures.World Trade Organisation system must levy duties on imports that are being dumped at extremely low prices because of the subsidies they are receiving from the Government. The increased imports at lower prices are injuring the native industries by causing less native production, reduction of employment and less margin of profits to cottage and Small Scale Industries.

Suggested Measures for Increasing Productivity of Manpower

1. Training in specific skills to individual workers. In any industrial unit registered with District Industries Centre.
2. Artisan training in specified industrial unit on specified trade.
3. Entrepreneurship training by District Industries Centre and NSIC.
4. Specific training on improved processes to the individual workers, supervisors and managers.
5. Common facility centres in all town Panchayats.
6. Assessment of the productivity of workers periodically by the Small Industries Service Institute (SISI).
7. Training in computer application to the managerial staff of Small Industries with minimum fees to be conducted in District Industries Centre.

Suggested Measures for Dispersal of Small Scale Industrial Activities

1. Industries are to be encouraged to be located in backward areas, hill areas and rural areas for reducing the regional imbalances. To encourage such a process the special incentives must be continued with more emphasis on newly designed incentives for backward areas, hill areas and rural areas. In such backward areas transport subsidy, power tariff subsidy, interest subsidy may have to continue till the areas are declared as developed areas on par with other areas.

Suggested Schemes and Programmes for 10th Five Year Plan period

Schemes for promotion of Small Scale Industries :

(1) Every Panchayat and Town Panchayat will earmark areas for industrial sheds and construct suitable sheds for occupation. Individual entrepreneurs may be encouraged to construct sheds with specifications without hindrance to the residential areas. Panchayats may plan to construct storage godowns facilitating small entrepreneurs. Village co-operative banks may be directed to issue industrial finance up to five lakhs and get them reimbursed form the commercial banks or SIDBI.

(2) Village Panchayats must develop marketing centres with showrooms for facilitating small entrepreneurs. The village Panchayats must plan for starting of Small Scale Industries in their areas either on co-operative venture or purely as Panchayat Industries to earn sufficient income to the Panchayat.

(3) The District industries Centre should develop testing laboratories and training facilities. The existing industrial estates are to be promoted with all infrastructure facilities and common facility centres. The District Industries Centre must co-ordinate in issue of finance, supply of raw materials and machinery, allotment of shed, training of personnel marketing facilities, assessment of schemes, sponsoring research projects, market net working and data base for export promotion with on line services. Every District Industries Centre must be facilitated with internet facilities for enhancing the flow of operation between import and export agencies.

Physical targets for 10th Plan period

The gross output of Small Scale Industries will have to be enhanced from 40 per cent to 75 per cent for solving the problem of unemployment in India. The Small Scale Industries sector should develop its employment potentiality to 200 million workers in the next ten years accomplishing a target of 100 million workers during the 10th plan period. In the case of export promotion, readymade garments, marine products and leather items may be given preference.

Investment level of Small Scale Industrial units

The investment for Small Scale Industries may be fixed at one crore for the purpose of extending all Government support. Any modernisation process must work with in the limit of one crore. Industries above one crore must stand on their own resources without special Government incentives.

Role of Agencies

The Government may urge the District Industries Centre to have clear and unambiguous district plan with assessment of resources, assessment of manpower, assessment of present industrial units, manufacturing units and fabricating service sectors, institutional finance available in the district; marketing facilities and net working. The District Industries Centre may have to pay sufficient attention on developing testing laboratories and for improving training facilities for workers, supervisors, managers and administrators.

The voluntary institutions may play a vital role in planning for the Panchayat areas, running production units, organising training programmes, building up storage facilities, taking up specialised research projects and so on.

The Panchayat Raj institutions will have to facilitate the Small Scale Units with allotment of plots, developing link roads, provision of water connections, issue of licenses and facilitating inter firm and inter departmental co-ordination. The small industrial association may have to concentrate on entrepreneurs experience sharing conferences, review meetings, seminars, symposia on advancement of technology and so on. The funding agencies such as commercial banks, SIDBI and others must be transparent in their dealings, so that, small entrepreneurs will have an easy access to them.

The state level technical and consultancy organisations may periodically review the progress of each industry in every district and list out the sick units for special care and revival measures.

Estimated Requirement of Industrial Finance

The estimated requirement of industrial finance will have to be prepared in consultation with the association of different industries for their requirements on infrastructure facilities, fixed assets, working capital loans and other schematic expenditures.

Innovative Financial Instruments for Raising Funds

The entire loan from the funding agencies may be granted and kept in the individual's account. The entrepreneurs may be allowed to with draw loan amount in different spells as and when required.

Requirement of Tools, Equipments and Machinery

The District Industries Centres must maintain the addresses of suppliers of machinery, equipments and tools. The companies who manufacture the machinery may also be advised to keep in touch with District Industries Centre. In addition to the individual requirements of machinery the District Industries Centre may establish common facility centres and testing facilities centres based on the needs in the district.

Existing Training Facilities

The NSIC, SISI and DIC's conduct training programmes in specialised industrial skills, managerial functions and in entrepreneurship development. Such training facilities may be extended to the voluntary and NGO's based on the facilities available with them.

Availability of Raw Materials

The village and tiny sectors mainly depend on locally available raw materials. The Small Scale Industries sector depend on inter regional or imported raw materials for some specific industries such as chemical industries, engineering industries, electronics and communicate and in pharmaceuticals.

The raw material supply should be ensured to the Small Scale Industries sector by the District Industries Centres and DIC's in turn are to be ensured by the NSIC.

Marketing Strategies

The traditional village industries generally undertake local and regional marketing. Modern tiny and Small Scale Industries sector produce for regional, inter-regional and international marketing.

For facilitating marketing the District Industries Centre may open a separate marketing wing under the supervision of a marketing manager with adequate godown facilities. The Tiny and Small Scale Industries sector may register themselves with the District Industries Centres for the regular quality of supply. In turn the District Industries Centres may register themselves with NSIC's for supply of goods to the Inter Regional or foreign market. The NSIC's may establish sufficient network with the export corporations in India and in other countries for supply and marketing of goods; the same line of service may be established for importing of raw materials.

Planning and Monitoring Mechanism

The planning of industries at District level will have to be done by the District Industries Centres. The monitoring also must be under the control of the General Manager, District Industries Centre thro' his inspectors.

Working of Existing Research and Development Institutions

The Khadi and Village Industries Commission has developed its own Research and Development Institutions in Wardha, Nasik, Bangalore, Ahmedabad and other places. The NSIC has developed Research and Development Institutions for Small Scale Industries sector in Okhla industrial estate, New Delhi. The Research and Development facilities are also developed by research institutions sponsored by the council for scientific and Industrial Research and Department of Science and Technology.

The universities and colleges may be given specific research projects on specific issues of industries and thus, the existing lab facilities in universities can be fruitfully used by utilising the manpower services of the research scholars. Ph.D. research topics can be sponsored by the CSIR and by DST, Government of India with Fellowship to the research scholars. A Directory of Research and Development institutions may be published by CSIR and copies may be made available The Principal, the Small Industrialists through District Industries Centres or through the Industrial Association. The Industrial Associations may have to strengthen their role in development of Research and Development in specific industries in different region.

Strategy for Export Marketing

The export oriented units of Small Scale Industries sector need the attention of the Government on priority basis. Special schemes maybe formulated for exporting units with specific financial support, technology upgradation, supply of scarce raw materials, quality assurance, packaging, marketing intelligence and infrastructure. The consortia of export units are to be encouraged to participate in international exhibitions. Marketing network and intelligence will have to be well advanced to keep up with the tune with the facilities with import and export agencies of other countries. In the context of the globalisation and liberalisation process will have to re-orient their productions and marketing strategies. As the share of the Small Scale Industries sector in import of the goods, some of the groups such as sports goods and ready made garments contribute between 60 per cent to 100 per cent. The finished leather and leather products contribute to 90 per cent. Processed food, rayon and synthetic fibre products contribute to the extent of around 60 per cent. Some of the areas such as auto parts, cycle parts, electronics, motorcycle parts, computer software, industries and readymade garments are some of the areas having very high export potentiality.

Areas such as quality of goods, infrastructure development, productions of labour, creation of brand name are to be attended in case for export units for improving their export potentiality. The Special Economic Zone's are Gujarat and Tamil Nadu for export oriented units. In the case of special Economic Zones, the government will have to consider certain specific aspects of development such as flexibility in labour laws, high quality of goods and removal of bureaucratic procedure.

Growth of Ancillary Units

Ancillary units which are taking partnership in production with the Large Scale Units are to be specially attended by the authorities with the higher capital investment and modernisation process. They should not be treated as mere Small Scale Units. They have to function as important segment in the production process to create World Trade

Organisation comparability. If these units are lagging behind without support and facilities, the export facilities cannot be strengthened to meet out the needs. Therefore, improvement of ancillary units would be highly essential.

Quality Certification for Small Scale Industries Sector

In quality certification process the CSIR and BIS will have to play a major role. There should be thorough check with regard to the quality of the products by the Bureau of Indian Standard. To ensure qualities CSIR will have to extend and establish the testing laboratories in all regions in all districts in association with District Industries Centres.

Implementations of the Recommendation of Earlier Study Groups

The task force may be constituted by the Department of Small Scale Industries and by the Khadi and Village Industries Commission to study the earlier recommendations, policy modifications and their effects and the impact of new policy measures.

Other Recommendations :

(1) Voluntary institutions must be encouraged to start Small Scale Industrial units with financial assistance and infrastructure facilities. Some of the enthusiastic institutions may run a cluster of industrial units for utilisations of resources and for providing employment to the local educated and unemployed.

(2) Village Panchayats may create marketing complex in their own areas for facilitating local marketing. Comparatively it will be easy for the Village Panchayats to develop infrastructure for marketing and thus, they will be able to generate income sources. The Panchayat Unions/Samithis may promote rural industrial estates with 10 to 20 sheds for facilitating new entrepreneurs to establish industries. The Panchayat Samithis may draw finance directly from SIDBI for infrastructure development in rural industrial estates.

(3) The District Development Councils may have to periodically discuss the District Plan and review the progress of work. The General Manager, District Industries Centre will become answerable to the District Development Council.

(4) In all district the District Industries Centres are to be strengthened with adequate powers to plan, to issue licenses, to supply raw materials, to supply machinery, to arrange for finance, to organise training, evaluate progress, to attend to marketing of products, and for promoting market intelligence including export promotion. The General Manager, District Industries Centre may have to be in the cadre of a Joint Director enjoying all the powers of Director of Industries at the district level. The Director of Industries may conduct periodical review meeting at least once a month with the General Managers and other supporting agencies.

4

Quality of Khadi Textiles :

Measures for Improvement

R. SEERANGARAJAN

Introduction

"Khadi" is a hand spun and hand woven textiles. Perhaps the hand spinning and hand weaving were among the earliest creative activities of the man to cover his body and protect from the climatic variations. Khadi was a symbol of Prestige of the Nation and a largest employment generation platform in the organized sector. Khadi will have to stay in India and there cannot be a second option about this. It can only be the remedy for growing unemployment problem of India and the khadi production tools are simple to operate with low technical input. Khadi promotes self-reliance, self-sufficiency and could be identified with the poor. It is a hard truth that there are millions of hungry mouths and unemployed hands waiting to derive succour through khadi. In fact it has generated employment to about 9,56 lakh persons during 2000-01 by producing only 0.5 per cent of total Indian clothing requirements. Employment statistics of khadi is furnished in Table 4.1 indicating its role in providing a meaningful earnings to khadi artisans across the country.

It is disheartening to find that khadi production has become stagnant or decreasing from Table 4.1 affecting the prospects of khadi activity despite its role, pride and prestige in Indian freedom struggle. There are several reasons attributed to its falling production like, quality not up to the mark, poor marketing, non-availability of rebates throughout the year, high cost factor and rigid pricing strategies. Of the above factors, prime responsibility is attached to the quality of khadi textiles affecting the durability and serviceability of the goods in use by buying a khadi material.

Table 4.1 : KVIC: Value of Production and Employment generation.

Sl. No	*Year*	*Employment in khadi in lakh persons*	*Quantity of khadi production in million sq. metres*
1	1991-92	14.20	109.10
2	1992-93	14.45	105.30
3	1993-94	13.87	98.40
4	1994-95	13.19	90.80
5	1995-96	13.97	105.10
6	1996-97	14.79	111.50
7	1997-98	14.01	104.20
8	1998-99	13.85	98.30
9	1999-2000	12.35	84.63
10	2000-01	9.56	69.39
11	2001-02	8.48	58.90
12	2002-03	8.58	62.03

Source : KVIC Annual Reports, Mambai.

Quality

Quality is the combination of several characteristics. The finally decided on is mostly a compromise based on circumstances. Quality is also defined as a "standard or excellence" possessed by an article or a product that meet the standards of performance characteristics or that meet customer requirements. Quality management deals with four "M"s, namely, materials, machines, men and methods. Thus, quality is a managerial function that involve all the people in the manufacturing organization. Quality is obtained out of excellent workmanship, care and experience in the art of manufacturing.

Quality of Khadi Textiles

Khadi fabric requires drastic improvement in the quality. Quality starts from fibre to fabric dyeing and finishing. For e.g. the cotton/polyester/ wool/silk raw material goes thro' the following processes.

(1) Fibre selection
(2) Spinning
(3) Weaving
(4) Scouring and bleaching
(5) Dyeing and printing
(6) Garment making

Quality of khadi products depend on the efforts taken in quality production at each stage of the above flow process chart. The khadi yarn quality much depends on the choice of the fibre used in spinning at mixing. Once the count to be spun has been decided, it is necessary to decide on the choice of cotton fibres to be used. A single measure namely, "Fibre Quality Index" has been evolved by the Textile Research Association, which will be helpful in choosing right fibre mix to achieve the desired yarn quality. The fibre parameters that ultimately decide the khadi yarn and fabric quality are, (i) fibre length, (ii) fibre fineness, (iii) fibre strength, (iv) fibre maturity and short fibre content.

Of the above, fibre length of cotton varies from 20 mm to 42 mm and the price of the cotton is determined by the length, namely, effective length, mean length or 2.5 per cent span length, etc. And fibre length determines the suitability of a cotton to spin the given count of yarn. It is also necessary to select fibre which has less variability in the length parameters and with lesser short fibre content.

Strength of the fibre is one of the vital parameters that reflect the durability of the khadi textiles. One of the major issues affecting khadi sales and customer acceptability is khadi fabric strength and durability. Choosing right fibre mix that meet the strength requirements of yarn and fabric will be done thro' stereometer, a fibre strength testing machine. Khadi institutions should adopt testing of fibre length and fibre strength at a nearby Textile Research Association or the field level testing wing of the Textile Committee, GOI.

Fibre fineness determines the suitability of a given fibre to produce different textile materials having variable fineness and texture. A soft texture require fine fibres while a coarse or thick texture requires coarser fibres. Thus, measurement of fineness of the given textile fibre assumes greater significance in producing khadi fabrics of desired fineness.

And trash content in the cotton determine the yarn appearance. Yarn appearance affect fabric appearance. Trash particles produce block spots on fabric surface. Therefore, while purchasing the cotton, the processing units have to ensure low level of trash per cent in the cotton thro' appropriate checking. Accordingly the beating points in blow room and waste extraction levels in carding machine have to be decided for better yarn appearance.

In processing of fibres to produce yarns and thereafter fabrics from yarns, efforts must be directed to produce quality outputs in work-in-progress stages. Online quality control measures are to be established thro' construction of quality control charts and periodical testing. Supervisors managing the khadi spinning and weaving centers have to pay continuous and consistent attention to all stages of processing including men and methods. Periodical maintenance of processing tools, cleaner methods and right handling of the tools and materials are to be ensured.

Charkha spinning is adopted in khadi sector to produce khadi yarn. The quality of khadi yarn produced is dependent on the drafting system used in the charkha. It influences mainly evenness and strength. Further, settings, choice of draft, selection of correct individual elements and maintenance of charkha also influence the quality of yarn produced. It also has effect on the spinning economics also yarn end breakages rate in charkha machine. Excessive drafts also reduce quality of the output yarn.

Factors Affecting Khadi Yarn Strength Quality of Drafting and Variable Settings in the Drafting Systems

Most of the charkhas use conventional drafting system and these outdated systems produce yarns at low quality. Khadi yarns have low strength that affect the quality and strength of the fabric. Newer and updated top arm drafting will give stronger yarn from charkha. Provisions must be available in charkha frame to change the break draft. A break draft of 1.3 - 1.5 will yield better yarn and smaller sizes of apron spacers will yield stronger yarn. Periodical maintenance of the drafting unit will ensure better quality of the yarn.

Charkhas have fixed settings in between the drafting rollers. And they are supplied to spinners to produce different counts of the yarn ranging from 33s metric to 92s metric. 33s metric yarn use cottons having effective length 23 mm (y-1,J-34) while 92s metric yarn use cotton having effective length of 33.5 mm (Suvin and Varalaxmi). If both cottons are processed in a charkha having fixed settings, it will yield weak yarns. Hence, provisions must be made to change settings in the charkha according to the type of cotton processed and count being spun. Apart from the above, periodical checking of the quality of khadi yarns must be undertaken to identify the faults and to make appropriate corrective action.

An important aspect of fabric quality that determines its visual rating is the uniformity of the cover between small areas of the order of 5 sq.cms. and lack of this uniformity gives rise to "patchy" fabric. Patchiness is basically the result of poor yarn quality, besides resulting in poor performance in reeling, warping, weft winding, weaving and in dye-uptake. All of the above are due to unevenness of khadi yarns. Before correcting unevenness, one has to assess the type; whether short term (within 50 cm lengths), medium term (50 cm – 100 cm length) or long term (above 100 cm lengths) variations. In textiles unevenness is usually expressed as C.V per cent or U per cent . This could be assessed by "uster" evenness testers. They produce the output in the form of spectrographs through which fault area could be located easily and corrective action is initiated. The spectrograph store informations on yarn thickness over several minutes and analyse the thickness profile for the presence of periodicities. Hence khadi yarns must be sent for "unevenness" tests to evaluate the faulty areas and to correct the same for producing better quality yarns. Short fibre content in the fibre influences khadi yarn unevenness. Higher the short fibre percentage, more is the floating fibres at each drafting zone and the more contribution towards quasi-periodic irregularity of yarns. Therefore, efforts must be made to remove short fibres in carding through better fibre individualization and effective extraction of flat strips. Combers are used to remove short fibres. Further, right choice of processing parameters from blow room to charkhas have influence to control yarn irregularity.

Thick and Thin Places

Thick places are visibly seen in charka spun khadi yarns. They are mainly due to the presence of unopened fibre individualization prior to drafting. And the second major cause is the irregularities during drafting in various machineries. It is worth to mention that number for thick places equally produce thin places in the yarn. Hence, it is suggested to maintain low level of production rate in cards to increase the rate of fibre individualization in case of finer count spinning in charkhas.

Secondly, emphasis on proper maintenance and right settings and choice of break drafts in the drafting units of charkha is to be made to reduce the occurrence of thick places in khadi yarns. A simple rule to find where the fault occurs is that if the difference between thick places and thin places per km is low, charkha drafting units must be checked. When the difference is more adequate attention is paid to carding and combing.

Neps in Khadi Yarns

When we observe the khadi yarns, we could observe quite higher number of small fibre knots called "neps". Neps may be "fibrous" or "foreign matters" based. These neps damage the appearance of khadi fabric and affect dyeability. The factors responsible for neppy yarn are, (i) nepping tendency of few finer varieties of cotton, (ii) harsh treatment at blow room, (iii) very closer setting at carding, and (iv) lack of maintenance in cards, combers and other machinery in processing. Periodic attention has to be made to select right number of beating points, truing the beater blades and ducts reconditioning in blow room. In carding, setting between cylinder and doffer should be near to 0.004", tuning the wire points with proper stripping and grinding schedules, and increasing the flat strips and rates of production. Similarly draw frames at rare situations generate neps due to scratches in creel table, high air currents and other punctures in drafting rollers. It is also pointed out that, that the effect on fabric appearance of high values of unevenness and thin places can be counter acted by a high cover factor the fabric, that neps cannot be. Therefore, nep control becomes even more important in khadi yarn production.

Hence, a plan of corrective actions has to be listed and carried out to improve the quality of khadi yarns.

Khadi yarn from charkas is mounted in a handloom in the form of warp beam. These warp threads form the longitudinal threads and weft yarn forms the crosswise threads in the interlacement process to produce khadi fabrics. While weaving also defects may appear on the fabric. The major weaving defects are reed marks, variations in pick density, shade variations in case of coloured fabrics, warp streaks, weft streaks and short piece lengths. Khadi weaving units should ensure better quality of khadi fabrics by enforcing quality drive among khadi weavers and artisans. In practice, the following defects appear or generated while making khadi fabrics in looms :

(i) *Oil stains on fabric surface* **:** Improper material handling by the weavers should be controlled.

(ii) *Zig zag selvedges* **:** Irregular tension during weaving will produce such selvedges. Warp and weft tension should be made even and just.

(iii) *Irregular reppiness* **:** Prominence of alternate picks in the fabric affecting uniform surface appearance. This can be prevented by ensuring right tension of warp during shedding and use of emery roller in take up.

(iv) *Weft snarls* : Caused by shuttle fly and rubbing of weft threads between shuttle and shuttle box base.

(v) *Weft bar* : A dark band across the width of the fabric showing prominence in the fabric. It can be controlled by using better 5 per cent yarn, avoiding count mix up and controlling tension in weft winding and dye variations in weft winding and the weft yarn packages.

(vi) *Floats* : In the absence of proper interlacements of warp and weft in certain cases, a float is formed over fabric. Entangled warp, held damages, very low warp tension have to be avoided.

(vii) *Weft slough off* : A weft slough off occurs due to improper tension in weft winding, high density coils, short chase lengths and over filled pins.

(viii) *Temple marks* : Appearance of definite marked holes the selvedges due to temple rod pins. May appear prominent in light woven woofer fabrics. Selection of right temples and avoiding the use of damaged temples will help in reducing temple marks.

Hence quality control measures are to be undertaken to avoid the above stated defects that will improve khadi fabric quality, thereby enlarging the marketing, generating more employment and better returns for the institutions working in khadi production.

REFERENCES

1. Foster (GAR), *Principles of Roller Drafting and the Irregularity of Drafted materials*, (Manual on cotton spinning), Vol. IV, Part – I, Textile Institute, London, 1958
2. Bandyopadhyay et al, *Imperfections in Cotton Yarns: Assessment and Census*, Proceedings of All India Textile Conference, 28th, 1971, p. 35
3. Udyog Pagati, *Special Issue on Quality*, NITIE, Mumbai, July – December 1986
4. Garde A.R. and Subramaniam T.A., *Process Control in Spinning*, ATIRA Publication, Ahmedabad, 1987
5. Ratnam T.V. and et al, *Norms for Spinning Mills*, SITRA Publications, Coimbatore, 1993.
6. Dr. N. Meenakshi Sundaram & Dr. R. Seerangarajan, *Developmental Strategies for Small Enterprises*, Gandhigram, May 2002.
7. Arindam Basu & Rajamma L. Gotipamul, *Quality of Indian and Some Imported Cottons*, Journal of Textile Association, Mumbai, July – August 2002, p.89

5

Marketing Management in Rural Industries

S. RAMESH BABU

The economic development of India is contributed by agriculture, industry, service sector etc. In the case of industries, it consists of Rural and Small Industries, Medium Enterprises and Large Scale Industries. Rural and Small Enterprises contributed nearly 40 per cent of the total production in the industries. These rural enterprises are highly suitable to India and other developing countries as this sector requires low capital, intermediate technology, capable of producing consumer oriented articles and can provide employment to rural people. Now the rural industries have attracted Women Self Help Group, young educated and uneducated entrepreneurs producing products such as Khadi and Village Industries, Coir, Handloom, Handicrafts, Sericulture, etc. The KVI products to the extent of Rs.10,000 crores is targeted for Tenth Five Year Plan period. The Government is extending positive assistances for rural industrial development through various all India Boards. But those who are managing this sector need to concentrate on marketing the products will have to concentrate on marketing management strategies which will make the products saleable. And thus rural industries sector can be more viable and successful.

Concept of Marketing

Marketing is very much integral to market. Market is a place where the sellers and buyers assemble to exchange their products for money and *vice versa*. Production precedes marketing. Production has undergone changes from time to time with changing business environment. Accordingly, the concept of marketing has also altered from one point of time to another. These concepts are broadly classified into two categories :

1. Traditional Concept
2. Modern Concept

These are discussed one by one.

Traditional Concept

This concept corresponds to the early production phase when there was a general scarcity of manufactured goods in the market. Then, the major function of marketing was to make the products widely available to the customers at an affordable price. The concept of marketing was held accordingly. Look at the following definitions to have the viewpoint of the traditional concept of marketing. Converse, Huegy and Mitchell observe :

> "Marketing includes activities involved in the flow of goods and services from production to consumption."

According to American Accounting Association, "Marketing is the performance of those business activities that direct the flow of goods and services from producer to consumer or user".

Thus the traditional concept of marketing is product-oriented.

Modern Concept

With the passage of time, the industrial activity intensified in terms of quantity, quality and variety of the products. This made the customers more sharp-sighted and choosier ones. Now, the customers were not ready to buy whatever was offered to them by the producers. They started to buy the goods or services that were more beneficial to them in terms of quality, price, satisfaction, durability, look and so on. The benefits to the consumers may be tangible and intangible. Therefore, the producers were compelled to produce what the customers want. Thus, a new approach, of course more scientific, emerged. The new approach relies on to produce the goods or offer services that satisfy the customers' demands. It is also termed as marketing orientation.

This modern concept of marketing can be understood in a better way by going through the following definitions.

According to Stanton, "Marketing is a total system of interacting, business activities designed to plan, price, promote and distribute what satisfying products and services to present the potential consumers".

Kotler opines, "Marketing is a social and managerial process by which individuals and groups obtain what they need and want through creating and exchanging products and values with others".

Now, we can easily distinguish between the two concepts. While the traditional concept of marketing focuses on the needs of the producers, *i.e.*, the seller, the modern concept concerns the needs of the consumer, *i.e.*, buyer.

Problems of Marketing

Production is the servant of market. Production is meaningless without market. Therefore, the very purpose of an enterprise is to produce what the customer will buy. All industries whether small or large face problems in marketing their products or services. But, small scale enterprises are more plagued by the marketing problems. In India, the utter failure of small-scale enterprises on the front of marketing of their products is commonly noticed over time and clime. Notwithstanding, there are two main reasons conditioning the marketing of products produced by small enterprises. First, small enterprises cannot withstand the cut-throat completion in respect of quality, cost, standardization of the products with medium and large scale industries. In fact, the same is attributed to one of the major reasons limiting the fuller utilization of their production capacity. Second, the small enterprises of our country neither have the full appreciation of the importance of marketing nor had they employed and implemented effective marketing techniques in their enterprises.

In this regard, the observation made by the Ford Foundation seems worth quoting :

> "In spite of an extensive potential market, the Indian small entrepreneurs were most reluctant towards efficient marketing technique and consequently have met with failure on the front of marketing of their products. When it comes to the question of markets for which the products are produced, most of the small entrepreneurs appear to be as much anchored to the past as they

are in the methods of manufacturing. Types and areas of consumption are shifting but only a few products try to follow them. This, in part at least, is due to the prevailing system of distribution. Few channels of communications exist between the small manufacturer and the ultimate customer. In many cases, the manufacturer does not even know in what part of the country his wires are used, or who buys them".

The Japanese delegation on Small Scale Industries in India also gave a similar view that the most knotty point in the operation of small scale enterprises and cottage industries is that the industry is isolated from the market and unable to understand quickly and accurately the prevalent trend of the market.

According to a field study of 50 small scale enterprises in a notified backward region of Uttar Pradesh, there are three major problems marketing of small industry products.

These are:

1. Competition with Modern Sector

The market competition of the small enterprises with the modern sector has aggravated due to several factors over the years, although the traditional hallmarks of the small scale industries are slowly yet steadily, changing there is an implicit assumption of poor quality for goods manufactured in small enterprises. This sector needs to cater to wide diversity and changing tastes and preferences of their clientele which they do fail.

2. Lack of Sales Promotion

Advertisement of the products through elaborate sales promotion methods such as cadres of trained salesmen, advertisement in cinema slides, posters, papers, magazines and so on has become increasingly fashionable particularly in the case of medium and large scale industries. But, Small Scale Industries lack in the required resources as well as knowledge to practice the methods of sales promotion. As a result, the former usually have patented names which facilitate the dealers in selling their products of Small Scale Industries, at least at their initial stage, persuasive capacity of the dealer plays and important role in influencing their sales. In such case, the dealers demand and producers are bound to pay a relatively higher rate of commission than those paid by the large-scale producers. This requires high unit cost and, thus, impinges on their capacity to compete with the large sector. In this way, the small enterprises are unstirred. If these small enterprises make a modest start too, it is to be stagnated and died out or devoured by the successful bigger enterprises.

3. Weak in Bargaining Power

In case of handicraft units such as copper smithy and carpet weaving units, the price realized is usually better when the sales are made at the place of production itself than when these products are marketed in the fairs. It looks that, very possibly, the manufacturers are in a better bargaining position at home than in other locations like fairs 'where they take their products for selling'. Other studies also support this finding.

One can add some other problems depending upon the type of enterprise, yet these are the major ones encompassing various problems in one way or other.

Market Assessment

You have understood marketing is to produce what the customers want. But it is not very easy to task to determine what the customers actually want. Any market is composed of a large number of customers/consumers with varying backgrounds like education, income, preferences, likes and so on. Further, these heterogeneous customers are spread over nearer and distant places of the enterprises. As a result, there is a wide variation in their wants. It is difficult, if not impossible, for a small scale enterprise to produce a variety of products to satisfy the varied wants of all the customers. That is why a small scale enterprise has to decide which group of customers, also called target segment, will be of particular interest to the enterprise. Having identified the target group of clientele to be served, the demand for the product by the target group can be estimated. Demand forecasting helps the entrepreneur in this task. Therefore, let us reflect upon what is meant by 'demand forecasting' referred to above.

Demand Forecasting or Market Demand

Before, we discuss demand forecasting, let us first understood what is meant by 'demand'.

The simplest and commonest definition of demand refers to the willingness and ability of customers to buy products or services. In other words, when the customers are willing and at the same time able to buy products or services, we say that there is a demand for the products or services. When we consider this definition for all the potential customers having both willingness and ability to buy a product, it is termed as 'Total Market'.

Considering that an enterprise has its own operational area, the definition of demand can be narrowed down accordingly. Based on it, have a look at the following widely accepted definition of 'market demand' given by Philip Kotler :

> "Market demand for a product is the total volume that would be brought by a defined customer group in a defined geographical area in a defined time period in a defined marketing environment under a defined marketing programme".

It follows from above definition that there are eight variables viz., product, total volume, bought, customer group, geographical area, time period, marketing environment and marketing programmes which must be well understood and taken into consideration while estimating 'market demand', also termed as 'demand forecasting'.

There are a number of techniques available for forecasting demand. The important ones are:

Survey Method

The survey method is the widely used method for estimating future demand of a product. This method is based on collection of date/ information from the potential customers, dealers and people with export knowledge about the subject. Under the survey method, if the number of respondents i.e., customers or dealers or knowledgeable person is small, all are surveyed, say information is sought from all. But, if the number is very large and all cannot be surveyed, only the representative number is surveyed or interviewed to collect the relevant information. This latter method is called 'sample survey method'.

Statistical Method

There are some statistical methods also *i.e.* 'time series analysis' and 'regression analysis' which are widely used for estimating the demand for the product. 'Time series analysis' is used where historical data on demand of the product are available to forecast the future trend. The use of 'regression analysis' is resorted to when there is a definite relationship between the relevant variable affecting the income and demand is established. For example, if the relationship between the customer's income and demand for a product is well established, 'regression analysis' may be used to estimate the demand for the product at various levels of consumer incomes. It is important to mention that some knowledge of statistics is necessary to make use of this method for estimating demand for the product.

Market Segmentation

You have just read that total market demand is composed of a large number of customers having different characteristics. Their demand for products, preferences, and liking with respect to prices, promotional strategies etc. vary. Thus, in order to tap the potential in different groups of customers, different marketing approaches need to be developed. For this, the customers with homogeneous characteristics from the heterogeneous market are identified. This exercise is termed as 'market segmentation'. Thus, market segmentation is an attempt to make the marketing strategies customer-oriented. Different people have defined market segmentation differently. Let us consider a few definitions given by different persons.

In the opinion of R.S.Davar, "Grouping of buyers or segmenting the market is described as market segmentation.

Philip Kotler opines, "Market segmentation is the sub-dividing of a market into homogeneous subsets of customers any subset may conceivably be selected on a market target to be reached with a distinct marketing mix".

To put in the simple words, market segmentation can be defined as the act of dividing the market into distinctive and homogeneous groups of customers.

The importance of market segmentation or target group is that it helps the entrepreneur in fine tuning his/her efforts to what the target group or customers want. Let us try to understand this through an example.

Suppose, Action Shoe Manufacturing Company want to identify its target group, i.e., customers. It specializes in shoes meant for men only, thus, excluding women from its target group. The shoes manufactured are expensive meant for men belonging to higher income groups and living in urban/city areas. In this case, the target group can be identified on the basis of three homogeneous characteristics of the customers: (1) men; (2) belonging to higher income groups; and (3) living in cities and urban areas.

Basis or Criteria of Market Segmentation

The market segmentation can be carried out on the basis of various defining, variables, viz., age, sex, education, income, geographical location, etc. Some commonly used bases/variables are:

(1) Geographical Variables
(2) Demographic Variables
(3) Educational Variables
(4) Income Variables
(5) Psychological Variables

A word about each of these variables will help us understand the identification of target group, i.e., market segmentation.

Geographical Variables

Geographical variations is an important variable in identifying market segmentation. The characteristics of the customers vary across the geographical locations. Hence, a firm need to classify its customers by the rural-urban origins. Because, the urban elite is generally highly educated and have high level of income. On the contrary, the rural mass is generally illiterate and its income level is woefully low. Similarly, some firm may target its efforts in one state, some other in few states, yet others in the entire country and still others may spread their wings across different continents. In all these cases, the geographical variables define.

Demographic Variables

Demographic variables include population variables like age, sex, marital status, number of children, etc. It is well-known fact that demand for products widely vary with regard to population variables.

An excellent example of demographic segmentation in the Indian Society is provided by population within age-group four to ten years can be easily correlated to specific products like toys, comic books and toffees. Thus, the demographic variables are commonly used as bases for identifying specific customer groups.

Educational Variables

It is confirmed that educational attainment and incomes are highly correlated. Education itself creates certain differences. For example, the reading habits of college students differs considerably from the high school students. On the whole, variation in the living styles of literate and illiterate people are quite visible. The proportion of literate population is quite small which varies across the States. Thus, the educational attainment of the population, i.e., customers becomes a sensitive basis for market segmentation.

Income Variables

Income of the customers provides an important basis for market segmentation. It is the level of income that influences the quantity and quality of products demanded. The levels of income vary considerably across places, occupations, educational attainment and so on. Further, the purchasing capacity of an individual depends upon the level of income. The customers' behaviour have a correlation with the income levels of the customers. The varying living styles of the American and the Indian, for example, supports and above fact. Thus, while introducing market segmentation, an entrepreneur has to concentrate on the levels of income of the consumers concerned.

Psychological Variables

Besides, the variables discussed above, there are some other variables also which relate to the psychology of the customers. These are, for example, personality, life style, tastes, interests etc., of the consumers. These outstanding psychological variables also bear outstanding values in segmenting a market. The best examples of psychographic market segmentation are goods made exclusively for status seekers with a high price tag attached to them like brief-cases, pens, watches, cosmetics and so on.

Marketing Mix

There are a number of aspects involved in marketing a product. Some of them are controllable and others are uncontrollable. The examples of controllable aspects may be the features of the product, its price, its selling through own salesmen or retailers, its advertisement through various means like television, newspapers and so on. In all these cases, there are a number of alternatives available to choose. The entrepreneur always tries to choose a mix alternatives/decisions amongst the alternatives which may yield the maximum returns for him/her. There are usually four main decision areas, *viz.*, product, price, promotion and place which constitute a mix of decisions. The same mix is termed as 'marketing mix'. McCharthy classified the four factor under 4 Ps, viz., Product, Price, Promotion and Place (Physical distribution).

The term 'marketing mix' was coined and introduced by Professor Neil H.Borden of the Harvard Business School. Both the term and concept have since been adopted throughout the world. Since, then, several authorities have tried to define this new concept of 'marketing mix' in different ways. Following are a few of them:

According to Prof. Borden, the term 'marketing mix' consists of the following:

(1) A list of the important elements or ingredients that make up the marketing programmes, and
(2) A list of the forces that bear on the marketing operation of a firm and to which the marketing manager must adjust in his search for a mix programme that can be successful.

R.S.Davar a well-known authority on marketing management opines. "The policies adopted by manufacturers to attain success in the market constitute the marketing mix".

Philip Kotler says, "the firm's task is to find the best settings for its marketing decision variables. The setting constitutes its marketing mix".

Thus, the marketing mix is the tailoring the product, its price, its promotion and distribution to reach the target customers. In the present time, marketing mix has become an essential part of marketing management.

The fair well-known of four Ps., *i.e.*, 'marketing mix' is shown in the Fig. 5.1.

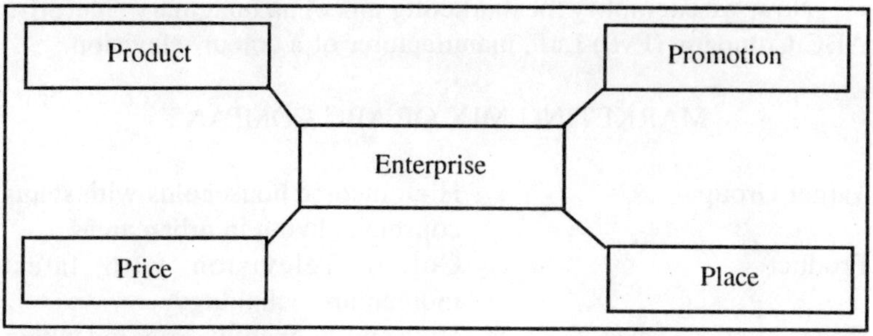

Fig. 5.1 : Marketing mix.

A word about each of these four variable will help us to understand marketing mix.

Product

The product consists of the policies and procedures relating the product times to be offered and services to be rendered. It also includes research and development programmes and the new product policy.

Price

This element of marketing mix consists of the policies and procedures relating to the price level, price specifications and the price policy.

Promotion

This element includes special selling plans or devices directed at or through the trade, form of devices for consumer promotions and trade promotions.

***Place* : (Physical distribution)**

This element includes policies and procedures relating to the channels to be used between the plant and the consumer, the degree of selectivity among wholesalers and retailers and attempts to co-operation of trade.

Price and place (physical distribution) are discussed in detail in the subsequent sections of the chapter.

Now, we exemplify the marketing mix of an imaginary enterprise ABC Company (Pvt.) Ltd., manufacturer of a colour television.

MARKETING MIX OF ABC COMPANY

Target Group	:	High income households with status conscious living in urban areas.
Product	:	Colour Television with latest indigenous technology
Price	:	High and competitive price but within the reach of people at the lower range of high income group
Promotion	:	Advertising through newspapers, magazines, radio and television
Place (Distribution)	:	Through reputed retailers in the urban areas

Marketing mix is bound to be different across the companies selling with different products. Marketing mix may also vary between the two companies selling the same product categories. For example, the marketing mix chosen by RMP Company may be substantially different from that of ABC Company mentioned above. However, these differences in their marketing mix are not anomalies.

Branding and Packaging

You have read certain aspects of a product, i.e., marketing mix. In fact, product presentation to the potential consumers is also an important aspect of product marketing. Branding and packaging are two aspects relating to product presentation. In this section, we would discuss these two important, of course, extrinsic attributes of a product, i.e., branding and packaging.

Branding

The word 'branding' has its origin to the word 'brand'. A brand is a name, word, symbol or a mark used to identify a product and to differentiate it from the competitive products. According to American Marketing Association.

> "A brand is a name, term, sign, symbol or design, or a combination of them, intended to identify the goods or services of one seller or group of sellers and to differentiate them from those of competitors".

Branding is a process of assigning a distinct name to the product so as to differentiate it from the competitive products of similar nature. If the brand is given a name, it is called 'brand name'. Example of brand names are Colgate tooth paste, Liril soap, Godrej refrigerator etc. In order to have a unique identity amongst the competing products, each brand is assigned a mark called 'brand mark'. A brand mark is a symbol or mark used for the purpose of identification of the product. Picture of an elephant in a distinct frame used by the Department of Tourism, Government of India and use of T in circle on buses and trucks made by TELCO are popular examples of brand marks.

When the brand name is registered under the Trade and Mercantile Marks Act, 1958, it is called 'Trade Mark'. A trade mark is the legalized version of a brand. Trade mark is shown by displaying the letter R enclosed in a circle.

Advantages

Branding offers distinct advantages to the buyers, the sellers and the society. Let us discuss them in detail.

Buyers

The buyers derive the following advantages from branding :

(1) A brand generally denotes uniform quality of the product.
(2) It makes purchasing easier and reduces the time and effort involved therein.
(3) Purchasing branded products gives psychological satisfaction to the buyer.

Seller

A seller also derives certain advantages from branding:

(1) Branding helps in identifying the product.

(2) It helps in carving out a niche for the product through differentiation.
(3) Branding helps in reducing selling costs by easing dependence on middlemen.

Society

Branding benefits the society also:

(1) Branding ensures quality of product.
(2) It helps in better dissemination of product knowledge.

Disadvantages

There is, however, an opposite view as well. Branding has certain disadvantages to the buyers sellers and society as a whole. These are as follows:

Buyers

Branding bears the following disadvantages to the buyers:

(1) Branded products become more costly to the buyers as brand development involves costs.
(2) Once the brand gains popularity, the manufacturer tends to reduce the quality of the product.

Sellers

Branding had the following disadvantages to the sellers:

(1) Developing and promoting a brand name involves money to be spent.
(2) Branding increases the cost of production leading to increase in prices.
(3) Seller finds it difficult to sell its product in the market amongst its rival products.

Society

The disadvantages of branding for a society are as follows:

(1) Branding often leads to higher costs and, in turn, higher prices. This is not considered as good from the society point of view.
(2) The brands enjoying the loyalty of the customers prevents the new producers from plunging into the market.

Packaging

Packaging is considered as an important element of product mix. Some marketers even consider it as a 'fifth P' along with product, price, promotion, and physical distribution. Packaging has been variously defined. One of the most quoted definition is "packaging is the art, science and technology of preparing goods for transport and sale". Thus, packaging has two salient aspects: (1) It helps in the physical distribution/transportation and sale of the products, (2) It performs the functions of selecting package design and packaging material. In other words, packaging means the activities of designing and producing the container or wrapper for a product. The container or wrapper is called the 'package'.

Packaging has emerged as an industry. It consists primarily of two distinct segments: (1) firms which manufacture material for packages, viz., paper, polyester, plastic, tin etc., and (2) firms which convert the packaging materials into packages. In addition, there are some other firms engaged in printing levels to be used in the packages.

Functions

Packaging should perform the following five functions:

(1) *Production*: Packaging should protect the product from damage in the process of transit, storage and use.
(2) *Appeal*: Packaging should attract and appeal to the customers. An attractive and appealing packaging serves as a silent salesman.
(3) *Performance*: The package must perform the test for which it is primarily designed. If the package fails to do so, the product itself becomes useless.

(4) *Convenience*: This is the fourth function of packaging. The package should be convenient to use, i.e., opening and closure of the package, the repetitive use valve, disposability, etc.
(5) *Cost-effective:* Finally, the package must be cost-effective also. While deciding on packages cost, costs incurred in storage and handling of the empty packages and filled packages, transport cost for distributing filled packages along with their insurance cost for the transit period, losses due to breakage or spoilage of the product etc., should be taken into consideration.

Advantages

Packaging offers the following advantages:

(1) It protects the product from damage in the process of transit, storage and use.
(2) A good packaging serves as a silent salesman and thus, promotes sales.
(3) It reduces the costs of transportation and storage of the product.
(4) Packaging helps in identifying the product and, thus, saves the customers from the use of duplicate and spurious products.

Criticism

Packaging is also subject to the following criticism:

(1) The consumers often throw away the empty containers in public places which causes environmental problems.
(2) The use of some plastic packaging and aerosol cans cause health hazards.
(3) Sometimes, packaging becomes deceptive when products of inferior quality are packed in attractive packages.

Legal Dimensions

Like other industries, the Government has laid down certain regulations in respect of packaging industry also. Principal among these is the product information given in the package known as 'levelling requirement'. Level is a display of written, printed or graphic matter on the package/container of the product. Levelling needs to fulfil the following statutory requirements:

(1) Net weight of the package when packed
(2) Date of manufacture
(3) Date of expiry
(4) Maximum retail price including or excluding local taxes
(5) Directives of use
(6) Directives of storage

A properly conceived level serves as an important sales instrument.

Pricing Policy

Once the production design is decided upon, the price of the product needs to be determined before selling it in the market. The enterprise has to take decision like at what price product will be sold out, how the price will be determined etc. Pricing policy help answer these questions. Therefore, what follows is meaning of price, its objectives considerations, policies etc.

Meaning of Price

Price, goes by various names - freight, fare, license fee, tuition fee, professional charge, rent, interest etc. But price in an enterprise/ business system is seldom so simple. By definition, price is the money that customers must pay for a product or service. In other words, price is an offer to sell for a certain amount of currency. Here, the word 'offer indicates that price is subject to change if there are found insufficient number of customers at the original price of product'. That is why prices are always on trial. If they are found to be wrong, either they must be immediately changed or the product itself must be withdrawn from the market.

Pricing of the product is something different from its price. In simple words, pricing is the area of translating into quantitative terms the value of a product to customers at a point of time. Someone has opined that "The key to pricing is to build value into the product and price it accordingly".

Pricing is one of the key elements of marketing mix. The salient ingredients of pricing are :

(1) Pricing covers all marketing aspects like the item – goods or services – mode of payment, methods of distribution, currency used etc.
(2) Pricing may carry with it certain benefits to the customers like guarantee, free delivery, installation, free after-sale servicing and so on.
(3) Pricing refers to different prices of a product for different customers and different prices for the same customer at different times.

Factors Affecting Prices

The prices that a firm can charge for its products are subject to many influences. The various factors – economic and non-economic – impinge upon the prices of the products. The important factors that may apply to all types of products are:

(1) Product Characteristics
(2) Product Cost
(3) Objectives of the firm
(4) Competitive situations
(5) Demand for the product
(6) Customer's behaviour
(7) Government regulations

One can classify the above factors into internal and external or controllable and uncontrollable factors. In our above factors, the first three factors can be classified as internal or controllable factors and the remaining four as external or uncontrollable factors.

A word about each of these factors will introduce us to the total scene of factors affecting prices.

Product Characteristics

By product characteristics, we mean numerous factors, i.e., the product life cycle, the product perishability, the product substitution and demand postponability or the magnitude of the resistance.

Product Cost

The second factor, the most important in determining price, is the cost of the product itself. While making marketing strategy, the decision makers should attempt to optimize the cost. The cost optimization helps in determining reasonable prices which provide equitable return on the cost employed *vis-à-vis* suits the customer's buying power. In order to optimize the cost of the product, the decision makers should study different types of costs, *viz.*, fixed cost, variable cost and incremental cost. These cost have already explained in an earlier chapter.

Objectives of the Firm

The objectives set by the firm also influence the prices of its products. For example, if the firm adopts skimming objectives, then the prices would generally be high. On the contrary, if the firm adopts the market penetration as its objective, the prices would normally be low.

Competitive Situation

The magnitude of competition in the market also affects prices. If the marketing manager finds that the magnitude of competition is high, prices would tend to be normally high. On the contrary, in the situation of low competition, the prices would to be higher due to favourable market environment. If competition exists between the product of the same line with similar quality, the marketer should also watch the prices of alternative/substitute products also while determining the prices of the competitive product.

Demand for the Product

The fact remains that among the various factors, the demand for the product concern is found exceptionally instrumental in guiding the pricing decisions. As per the law of demand, if there is more demand for the product, prices will be high and *vice versa*.

Besides, seasonal nature of demand can also affect pricing policy by making it possible to alter prices with the high and low seasons of demand for the product.

Customers' Behaviour

In making pricing decisions, the study of customers' behaviour bears relevance. Of late, the behavioural scientists have gravitated increasing attention on the behavioural science. They feel that an in-depth study of the customers' behaviour would help diagnose the reactions of the customers regarding a product. While studying customers, they should be traced out into specific groups in line with market segmentation discussed earlier. For example, if the marketing manager has to deal with the industrial consumer, the pricing decisions would be different. On the other hand, if he has to deal with the general consumers, the pricing decisions would be somewhat distinct.

Government Regulations

While deciding pricing policy, the decision maker does not need to under estimate the Government regulations imposed from time to time to control the business activity in the country. Therefore, due weightage should be assigned to such regulations like MRTP Act, Essential Commodities Act, Industries Development and Regulation Act, Consumer Protection Rights and the Defence of India Rules. The basic purpose of these regulations are to optimize and regulate the distribution of consumer goods.

Pricing Considerations

Unquestionably, the major objectives of pricing is the earning of maximum profits. This may be done by a pricing, policy that will attempt to achieve a high return. Whatever pricing policy is decided on, for maximum effectiveness certain considerations must be taken into account before prices can be set. Following are the important considerations weighed in the pricing of the product :

(1) Impact of price and output respectively on revenue and cost.
(2) The level of output that can yield the maximum contribution towards overheads and profits.
(3) Scope for price adjustment in accordance with changes in cost and demand conditions of the product.
(4) Investigating into future implications, if any, of price change.

(5) Recognition of rival's pricing strategies as well as quick reactions.
(6) Element of elasticity of demand and revenue.
(7) Effects of changes in prices of the product on the entry of the new enterprises.

Pricing Policies/Methods

The common pricing methods and strategies are discussed below:

Cost-plus Method

The cost involved in the production of any product becomes the prime basis for determining its price. This cost plus method is the commonest method used to pricing by the small-scale enterprises. According to this method, firstly, the total costs, i.e., fixed cost and variable costs are worked out. Then, a certain margin is added to total costs because the basic objective of running an enterprise is to earn profits. Now, what sum comes after is the selling price of the product. To put it in simple equation:

Total Cost (Fixed + Variable) + Profit = Selling Price

Skimming Pricing

Under skimming pricing strategy, a very high price is charged in the beginning with a view to recover the cost involved within a shorter period of time. This policy is feasible when the new product introduced is innovative and is used mainly by sophisticated group of customers. However, the high price is usually supported by heavy promotion. This policy cannot continue for a long period of time because high price of the product attracts other manufacturers/entrepreneurs also to plunge into manufacturing. As a result, the competition sets in and the prices fall.

Penetration Pricing

This is, in a way, contrary to the skimming pricing policy. Under this policy, the price of the product is set at a lower level to penetrate into the market. The underlying idea is to attract as many customers as possible at the very outset. This policy can be adopted when the customers are very particular for price and when the product is an item of mass consumption.

Market Rate Policy

This policy adopts the prevailing market rates for determining the price of the product. This method is used when the product is indistinguishable from those of the competitors. This method is also used in case of unbranded products like oils, courier, tailoring and repairing/servicing.

Variable Price Policy

Under this policy, the price of the same product varies from customers to customers depending upon the situation prevailing in the market. This method is adopted with an objective to maximize the profits. The following are some market situations when the entrepreneur adopts the variable price policy:

(1) There is difference in the size of customers (e.g. a lower price may be offered to bulk customers).
(2) There is difference in the demand and supply powers between the locations.
(3) There is difference in the bargaining powers of various customers.
(4) There is difference in the customers' ability to pay for the same product.
(5) There is difference in the knowledge of customers' about the market price of the product.

Resale Price Maintenance (RPM)

Under this policy, the manufacturers of the product fix prices for the wholesalers and retailers. The retail prices of the product like drugs and detergents are printed on the package. However, the retail price is fixed somewhat higher to meet the cost of inefficiency retailers not selling the goods timely. While its advantages are its freeness from competitions and no need for the customer to bargain, its main disadvantage is that it deprives of the customers from the advantages which may accrue to them through competition.

Distribution Channels or Methods of Marketing

Production is for consumption. Having produced the products, these need to be made available to the final users of the product, i.e., the consumers scattered in large geographical areas. Since, many a times it becomes extremely difficult, if not impossible, to reach the customers on its own, the firm needs the help of marketing intermediaries, like wholesalers and retailers, to reach their products to the ultimate/final consumers. These intermediaries serve as channels to reach the product to the consumers. Let us consider a few definitions on distribution channels.

According to the committee on Definitions of the American Marketing Association (1960):

> "A channel of distribution or marketing channel is the structure of intra-company organisation units and extra-company agents and dealers wholesale and retail, through which a commodity, product or service is marketed".

R.S. Devar observes, "Distribution as an operation, or a series of operations which physically bring goods manufactured or produced by any particular manufacturer into the hands of the final consumer or user".

In fact, channels of distribution are like pipelines which take the right quantities of the right product to the right location where the target consumers want them at the right time. This section, therefore, deals with the process how products go through this channel from the producer to the final user. These distribution channels, in a way, refer to the methods of marketing also.

In view of the number of intermediaries, distribution channels can be classified into three categories. These are:

(1) *Zero-Level Channel* : When the distribution of the product is direct from the producer to the consumer or user. This is also called direct selling.

(2) *One-Level Channel* : When the product it not sent direct from the producer to the consumer but the producer sells the

product to the retailer who, in turn, sells to the consumer. This channel is also known as distribution through retailers.

(3) *Two-Level Channel* : When there are two levels of different kinds of intermediaries between the producer and the consumer. In other words, under this channel, the manufacturer sells the product to the wholesaler who sells to the retailer and who finally sells to the consumer. This is called as distribution through wholesalers and retailers.

All these three channels can better understood with the following Figure also. Let us discuss these in some more details.

1. Direct Selling

Producer ⟶ Consumer

2. Through Retailer

Producer ⟶ Retailer ⟶ Consumer

3. Through Wholesalers and Retailers

Producer ⟶ Wholesaler ⟶ Retailer ⟶ Consumer

1. *Direct Selling*

This method is also referred to as producer to consumer channel. Under this channel, the producer of goods attempts to make a direct contact with the ultimate user of goods by several methods of selling including door-to door sales persons. This method is most common in industrial marketing particularly in respect of capital goods like industrial chemicals, heavy equipments etc.

Direct selling to the consumers has the following advantages to the producers:

(i) Close relationship to the consumers makes the producer constantly aware of changes and other consumer needs.

(ii) Profit do not go to the middle-man.

(iii) Goods get to the consumer more quickly because they do not have the travel through intermediaries or middlemen.

Despite these apparent advantages, direct selling has not become a powerful channel. According to an estimate, even less than 3 per cent of total consumer sales are made in this channel. This is to the following reasons:

(a) The producer has to spend a handsome amount in the training, maintaining and supervising a large number of sales staff.
(b) It involves cumbersome difficulties in providing and maintaining inventories of goods at many locations to assure prompt delivery to the customers.

2. *Producer to Retailer to Consumer Channel*

This is a kind of indirect selling. This channel avoids wholesalers. It is suitable when products are perishable and speed in distribution is extremely essential. The goods that are frequently sold in this channel are fashion merchandise, products requiring installations, high value goods, etc.

3. *Producer to Wholesaler to Retailer to Consumer Channel*

This channel is also known as the traditional channel. This is also the most common method of distribution under which the producer sells to the wholesaler, who, in turn, sells to the retailer, who finally sells to the consumer. In this system, the wholesaler is granted a certain portion of the total profit, in return for which he or she buys stores, sells delivers and extends credits. This channel is invariably used in respect of groceries, drugs, drug goods, etc. This channel option is particularly suitable to the following producers:

(1) Who lack in financial resources;
(2) Whose product line is narrow; and
(3) Whose products are not subject to fashion changes and physical deterioration but are durable.

Despite these features, this channel suffers from certain limitations also. To mention: (i) An over-dependence on wholesalers causes him/ her *i.e.* the producer to lose contact with the dealers, (ii) The wholesaler may have different products of different producers to sell. In such case, the wholesaler might be quiet unable to push up the sales on one specific product produced by a producer.

Despite the various merits and demerits of all the three above mentioned channels, the producer to wholesaler to retailer to consumer channel has been commonly used by most of the producers to distribute their product to the ultimate consumers.

After going through the above description, an inevitable question arises in the mind in which one is the best suitable channel for distributing the products of a small enterprise. Therefore, one last word on channel choice before we close this section.

How to Select a Suitable Channel?

The success or failure of an enterprise *inter alia* depends upon, to a great extent, the selection of a suitable channel of distribution. There are a number of factors that must be considered when a channel of distribution is to be selected. In practice, many choices are available, so a careful study is required before a decision could be reached that will fit to the specific conditions of the enterprise to be the best channel of distribution. Some of the important factors to be kept in mind while selecting a distribution channel are:

(1) Study the channels that are available, more especially those used by the competitors.
(2) Determine the channel that will best match the salient characteristics of the product to be marketed.
(3) Estimate the probable demand for the product.
(4) Consider the available financial resources.
(5) Approximate the costs, sales and profits for each available channel.
(6) Determine the size of the product line and amount of a typical order.

How much crucial the selection of a suitable channel of distribution is for new product of a small enterprise is well testified by a grape juice enterprise. The juice was originally sold through food brokers who delivered exclusively to warehouses and only replenished retailers' shelves once a month. This led to poor display and frequent out-of-stock situations. By replacing food brokers with distributors who delivered the beverage to stores several times a week. Thus grape juice producer transformed his marginal product into a highly successful one by selecting the most suitable channel of distribution for his (juice) product.

Government and Departmental Purchase

The success of an enterprise whether large or small, greatly depends upon their ability and efficiency in marketing their products. It has been well realised that the small-scale enterprises face several problems in marketing their products. Marketing assistance to these small units is thought to overcome their marketing problems. From this point of view, several agencies have been set up to offer marketing assistance to small-scale enterprises. The scheme of Government and Departmental Purchase is one of them. Let us discuss it in more details.

Central Government Stores Purchase Programme

In order to avail of this assistance, the interested small-scale enterprises are required to register themselves with the Director General of Supplies and Disposals (DGSD). The Stores Purchase Programme of the Central Government administered through DGSD provides a marketing outlet for the products manufactured by small-scale enterprises. The DGSD procures stores requirements of various central government departments, public sector organisations and semi-government bodies. But, if the small-scale enterprises are registered with the National Small Industries Corporation (NSIC), certain additional facilities are offered to them. For example, these are:

(1) Free registration with DGSD.
(2) Free supply of Tender Forms.
(3) Exemption from depositing security and paying earnest money.
(4) Price preference upto 15 per cent over the lowest quotation received from a large scale enterprise for the same product.
(5) Reservation of certain items (at present 409 items) for exclusive purchase from small-scale industries.

In line with above policy, the DGSD has classified the items for purchases by the Government Departments into the following six groups:

(i) Items which could be procured from large scale units and which have no concern to small scale units.

(ii) Items which can be manufactured by large-scale units but also permit scope for purchase of parts and components from small-scale units.

(iii) Items which could be produced by both large and small scale units. But, as mentioned products and small-scale units are given 15 per cent price preference over the price quoted by large-scale units for the same products.

(iv) Items which are reserved for exclusive purchase from small units.

(v) Items for which purchases up to 75 per cent are to be made exclusively from small-scale enterprises.

(vi) Items for which purchase up to 50 per cent are to be made from small-scale units.

Railways, Posts and Telegraphs and Defence

In order to help small-scale units in marketing their products, the Railway Board has introduced a scheme of providing preferential treatment to small-scale units since 1961. The small-scale units registered with the NSIC for participation in the Stores Purchase Programme have to apply to the Controller of Stores of each railway for departmental purchase. A price up to preference up to 15 per cent is given to the small-scale units registered with the Railway Board. The registered small units are the payment of earnest money and security deposit in respect of railway tender order.

Canteen Stores Department (India)

This is yet another Government Undertaking to purchase small-sector products. With its head office located at Bombay, its canteens are located at various cantonments and defense establishments. The CSD (I), Bombay purchases consumable articles in large quantities. The entrepreneurs who desire to market their products through this organisation need to contact the Canteen Stores in its head office at Bombay.

Purchase by State Governments

In view with the DGSD guidelines, the State Government have also come forward to help the small-scale units in marketing their products. Accordingly, the State Governments have given price preference to small-scale units ranging from 10 to 15 per cent in their purchase programmes. The highest price preference up to 17 per cent is given by Himachal Pradesh to its small-scale enterprises. The price preference is generally given to the small-scale units located in the particular state.

Sum Up

Production is meant for consumption/marketing. Marketing is a process of ascertaining the consumers' needs, converting them into product or services and moving the product or services to the final consumer to satisfy his needs and wants. Thus, the concept of marketing is customer-oriented, i.e., produce what customers actually want.

Marketing is an important is not so easy. Small Scale Enterprises face several problems in marketing their products. Competition with modern sector, lack of promotion and weak bargaining power are the major problems faced by small enterprises in marketing their products.

What customers want is ascertained by market assessment. Market assessment is done on the basis of demand forecasting. The major techniques used to forecasting demand are survey method, statistical method and leading indicator method.

The process of dividing whole market into distinctive and homogeneous sub-groups is called market segmentation. It helps tap the potential in different homogeneous groups of customers.

All marketing activities divided into four basic elements, viz., product, price, promotion and physical distribution, are referred to as the 'marketing mix'. These are also referred to as 'four Ps' in marketing.

A brand is a name, sign, symbol or design assigned to a product to identify it and to differentiate it from competitive products. Good branding serves as a silent salesman. Packaging refers to the activities of designing and producing the container or wrapper for a product. Packaging protects the product from damage in the process of transportation, storage and use.

Price is the exchange value of a produce or service. The important factors that affect the price of a product are product cost, demand and characteristics; firms' objectives; customers' behavious and government regulations. The principal pricing methods adopted in small enterprises are cost-plus method, skimming method, penetration method, variable price method, etc.

Channel of distribution refers to the network through which a product moves from the place of its production to the place of its consumption. Distribution channels create time, place and ownership utilities to the product. Channels of distribution are broadly grouped into two categories:

(i) *Direct Channel* : When the producer himself makes the product directly available to the customers, it is called 'direct channel' or 'direct selling'.

(ii) *Indirect Channel* : When the producer makes the product available to the customers through the middlemen like wholesalers and retailers, it is called 'indirect channel'. Both channels have their distinct advantages and disadvantages.

REFERENCES

1. Philip Kotler, *Principles of Marketing Management Prentice Hall,* New Delhi, 2000.
2. Rajan Nair, *'Marketing',* S. Chand & Co., New Delhi, 2000.
3. Stanton J., *Fundamentals of Marketing,* McGaw Hill, Inc., 1994.

6

The Environmental Challenges of Small Entrepreneurs

L. RATHAKRISHNAN

Introduction

Man has always been a part of nature and continues to be so. The confrontation between man and nature is an internal contradiction of a system in which man and nature are the two interdependent parts. The manifestations of this confrontation are two – the apparent supremacy of man gained over nature through his scientific inventions and technological break-through and the irresistible reactions of nature such as the ozone layer depletion, global warming, changing sea currents, and climatic changes.

The said confrontation is not a problem of science *perse* as perceived until now, but it is a problem of misuse of science against nature. The problem lies in thc changing socio-economic and cultural values of man. Consequently, the solution can possibly be seen in understanding man's traditional societal ties with nature and ethical value system. This paper examines the different environmental challenges faced by small enterprises in new millennium.

The environmental related problems have been noticed only in 19th century, especially from 1880 onwards. It is during this period that the industrial revolution started to take place first in England, European Union, America and the rest of the world. From this period the economists and other policy decision makers started to advocate 'Industrialisation strategy', which is *sine qua non* for economic development. Consequently the industrialisation strategy was adopted all over the world without understanding natural eco-system of the particular region. Hence, we face the present problem of environmental degradation and other environmental catastrophic issues. Although the large-scale industries are responsible for environmental related problems but the involvement of small scale industries can not be ignored. They are also responsible, partly for disturbing the environment. The small-scale leather industries for example predominantly pollute air, waterways, and soil. Hence, they should behave in such a manner that they must go for environmental friendly technology such as recycling, re-use, and no waste economy. This kind of change in attitude may bring better future and sustained industrial development.

Major Environmental Challenges

Environment and Development

The primary issue now is how to develop the economy without destroying the environment because environment and development are interdependent. Again environmental degradation occurs both due to lack of development as well as inappropriate development. It is difficult to develop an economy, particularly in the developing country like India without damaging environment. On the one hand all third world countries are aiming to attain higher level of GDP growth (6-8 per cent per year) and on the other the first world countries are striving for sustainable development through higher level of consumption. By using science and technology, the developed countries, strenuously trying to integrate the environment into industrial development besides introducing new strategies to internalise environmental externalities through life cycle assessment and industrial ecology.

Economic developmental activities have mostly destroyed our ecosystem. Modern technology and industrial development have greatly influenced sophisticated life of human beings as well as detoriating environment. The advanced medical facilities say for example improved health status and also increased demand for the products of nature. The pressure on natural resources destroys the eco-system and the environment.

The issue here is:

1. What is a real economic development?
   (a) is it sufficient to declare a country as advanced on the basis of Gross Domestic Product, per capita income, and higher standard of living? or,

   (b) should we incorporate the parameter such as rapid increase in population; poverty; decreasing quality of land, air, and water; decrease in the carrying capacity of the ecosystem; loss of bio-diversity; and climate change into our developmental indicators?
2. whether to preserve natural resources or destroy environment in the pursuit of economic growth?
3. do environmental problems really affect economic development or to what extent environmental problems affect economic growth?
4. is there any way to improve the betterment of human beings without degrading natural resources?
5. can we imagine industry free but only resource based economic development?
6. how economic growth has been affected or slowed down by the severe consequence of environmental problems?
7. how to integrate the environment into small enterprise development, although they are not fully responsible for degrading environment ?
8. who is the real culprit for environment problems ?
9. does the growth of population affect the progress of small entrepreneurs ? and,
10. what kind of small enterprises grow or degrade due to heavy population explosion?

Industrialisation led Urbanisation

Industrialisation and subsequent development are the main cause for urbanisation. When people start to migrate from village to urban centers they may cause severe environmental problem in urban areas. Sanitary conditions will be poor, solid waste remains unremoved, food and drinking water will be contaminated, noise level will also be higher. All these environmental problems affect the lives of the urban population. The urban waste disposal dumped in open places spoil the surface, ground water, land, and air. Most of the industrial wastage is toxic and hazardous, which was sent by them to the environment, untreated. These unhygienic practices in urban areas spread diseases. Studies have estimated that 85 per cent of water discharge brings infectious diseases such as diarrhea, malaria, and gastroenteritis. In addition, urban slums also spread several ailments, namely communicable diseases, malnutrition, mental and physical retardation, and behavioural problems.

The issue here is:

(1) how to control the fast spread of urbanisation?
(2) in what way industries in general and small enterprises in particular play an important role to reduce urban congestion?
(3) how decentralised industrial location helps in arresting migration of people from village to urban areas? and,
(4) what is the role of small entrepreneurs to solve the problem of urbanisation and poor urban sanitation?

Industrialisation

Industrialisation is considered as *Sine quo non* for economic development irrespective of resource availability and technological progress of a country. In fact, industrialisation has brought immense benefit to the humankind but they have also brought new dangers, largely through waste generation and the manner in which the industrial waste is disposed. Very little is known about the long-term consequences of man's exposure to all types of toxic wastes. Unless proper planning and management strategies are implemented while establishing industries, the general standard of environment will continue to deteriorate concomitantly bringing serious health problems to all living things, close to industrial area. Development of new technologies, environmental auditing, life cycle assessment, and industrial ecology are new strategies to achieve sustainable development of the economy. For example the Tamil Nadu newsprint and paper limited has used bagasse (sugarcane waste) as raw material for producing paper. They do not relay on chopping down trees for paper production. These responsible manners of action helps for conserving of 30,000 acres of forest land every year. This kind of attitude not only helps forest conservation but also solve the problem of waste disposal from sugarcane industries. This kind of activity is called as industrial alternatives to shrinking forest cover and declining wood availability.

However, paper industry also create some environmental problems such as air pollution (smoke and dust), soil waste, and effluent waste. For instance chlorine usage in bleaching, produce toxic material and solid waste generations are other environmental problems associated with paper manufacturing. Therefore, the paper industry have to respond in such a manner that all pollution preventive strategies have to be adopted. They can use hydrogen peroxide for bleaching pulp instead of chlorine, which is toxic. The industry should also try to reduce solid waste generation. Full fledged effluent treatment plant had to be installed in the industry to treat all used water. Similarly, chimneys height have to be increased and the entrepreneurs have to take steps to re–use all solid waste, while making paper.

It is a known fact that Government effort was main reason for the domination of small-scale industries in India. Again the very same Government policy was responsible for declining the proportion of workforce engaged in traditional forest based industries. The industrial motives of forest clear felling and conversion of mixed forests into monoculture plantation have led to inestimable rural poverty and unemployment. Due to over exploitation, some of the rich bamboo stock in forest become totally barren.

The leather industry is another small-scale industry face the problem of effluent disposal. This industry is also called as 'pollution intensive industry'. The large scale tanning operation can lead to eroding of soil. It is due to discharge of many toxic pollutants like sulfide, chromium and other mineral salts, dyes and solvents. Most of the tanneries in India are century old with no drainage facilities having inadequate measures to recycle or diffuse the effluents. Due to non-adoption of effluent treatment plants many small entrepreneurs in tanneries sector have been closed. The tannery industries problems are severe in place like Kanpur, Agra, Lucknow, Kolkata, Vaniyampadi, Vellore and Dindigul. Non of the old tannery systems have filtering the air mixed with nitrocellulose, lacquer and other chemicals, spread in the process or most sophisticated leather using resin binders. Unless sufficient efforts has been paid on treating waste effluent, the small scale tannery and leather industry may not have smooth going in future, in the face of stringent pollution control measured adopted by the Government of India.

Industrial effluents are greatest danger for water contamination. The process of rapid industrialisation have always discharge toxic chemicals effluents to various water sources like streams, rivers and tanks, causing serious damage to water quality and contamination of ground water. As industrial waste contain chemicals and having metals such as arsenic, lead, mercury, cadmium and zinc, which are harmful to human health and eco-system. When this water was used for irrigation, polluted water has serious impact on land productivity, food chain, human and animal health. The dying units in Tirupur are best example in Tamil Nadu. These enterprises cause land degradation, pollute soil, contaminate water and other health related problems to the local people.

Therefore, it is mandatory for the industries to adopt some environmental regulations and go for environmental friendly technology or measures to contain all environmental problems.

The important issues are:

- what are the linkages exists between industrial development and changes in the micro-environment ?
- what type of damage is taking place to crops and animal husbandry due to industrial pollution?
- how industrialisation strategies influence on health and sanitation of rural communities as well as the urban environments ?
- how to identify suitable industries for development of particular region or a country?
- what kind of technology is need for Third World Countries, either labour intensive or capital intensive or the so called appropriate technology for industrial development?
- when the socialistic countries are moving towards globalisation and want to be a member of WTO, how can the interest of Third World be neglected in the context of maintaining international pollution standards?
- when the word 'competition' is a big term for big industrialists, how to make the term more friendly to small scale industries?
- when the investment and all associated parameters are small as compared to large-scale industries, how the small enterprises adhere the rules and regulation of WTO as well as the Central or State pollution control board of India?
- how to bring environmental regulations to the competitiveness of polluting industries?
- how to change the attitude of competitive position of polluting industries?
- what are the factors to be examined while diffusing cleaner technology to small-scale industries so as to make these industries as environmental friendly?

- how to standardise the polluting industries ? And can we bring the same kind of pollution prevention norms similar to that of advance countries?

Industrialisation and Pollution

Pollution arises due to population growth and subsequent agricultural and industrial activities. Each year we are adding 0.2 per cent of CO_2 into the atmosphere. In addition, atomic energy and thermal power also pollute environment. Since pollutants are globally distributed their harmful effects appear at long distances from the points of origination. Though developing countries are not the major contributors of pollution they can be severely affected by the problem of 'Transboundary Pollution'. The USA, European Union, and Japan produce more than 40 per cent of global CO_2 emission (Anon 2000 b:1). Due to polarisation effect industries are concentrating in certain specific locations. This again causes concentration of polluting elements in air, water, and land.

Now the issues is:

- although various legislation's have been enacted in the country for controlling the pollution, how far this has been followed or adopted? The reduction in pollution level is possible only by self-imposed discipline on the part of industries and transfer of clean technology to the third world countries without any conditions.
- how to keep away the small entrepreneurs from producing polluting elements in to the atmosphere.

Industrialisation and Land Degradation

With the increase in population, most of the cultivable area had been diverted to non-farm activities. In order to increase agricultural production, farmers are practicing various farm technologies in their limited farm size. Use of fertilisers and pesticides, for instance adversely affects the nature of land, and degradation becomes unavoidable. Over two million hectares have been degraded, which could be reclaimed through appropriate wasteland reclamation measures. This could help to boost agricultural yield and simultaneously reduce unemployment and poverty.

Mis-use of land, incorrect methods of disposal of solid and liquid waste, and increased amount of waste generated through domestic, industrial, and agricultural practices greatly cause soil pollution. Industries are also responsible for degradation of land and soil infertility. Small scale Industries, though small in investment and less operational area but they also produce huge toxic and other unwanted polluting elements in to the land, soil, water, and air. For instance, leather tanning and textile dying industries are greatly cause and pollute the environment. In the event of untreated waste water and solid waste, it harms land, soil, water bodies, flora, and fauna. It also adversely affect the health of human beings.

In order to reduce land degradation, the small-scale entrepreneurs should adopt the following measures :

- contain and regulate the waste disposal especially the waste disposed on land. All toxic elements should be removed from industrial waste before disposing into open space.
- try to locate the environment polluting industries away from residential areas and away from riverside.

Deforestation, Bio-diversity, and Species Extinction

Deforestation has risen due to excessive felling of trees for timber, over grazing, fire, and clearance of land for cultivation and pastures. Obviously all these activities are taking place at an alarming pace in the developing countries. Forests are vanishing at the rate of 17 million hectares per year, an area of about half the size of Finland. The issues related to deforestation continue to cause great concern to the world community because the destruction and degradation of forest cause soil erosion and also disturb the water resources. It is estimated that about 6000 million tonnes of topsoil with all essential nutrients are flowing into the sea every year (Khan, 1999: 193). This topsoil removal has been heavily affecting the tribal economy in addition to siltation problems in reservoirs and dams. Since deforestation disturbs ecological balance and deteriorates quality of life, it was discussed at great length as the Rio Summit in 1992.

Deforestation is a major cause of loss of bio-diversity and species extinction. Some of the life forms have totally vanished while some others are categorised as endangered. About 3120 species of plants and 172 categories of animals of our country are listed in the IUCN's Red List threatened category.

It is often said that industries are held responsible for deforestation, loss of bio-diversity and species extinction due to industrial use of hard and softwood for various purposes. The New Forest Policy of India and the rest of the world have either banned cutting or felling of green trees or asked to go for scientific method of harvesting trees and scientific management of forests. As the requirement of round wood is growing year after year the illegal method of cutting trees still continues all over the world. In some other cases the large-scale industries located in developed countries receive wood from less develop countries by offering AID to them. In the process they try to protect their native forests at the same time sustained survival of forest industries in their own country and induce deforestation in Third World Countries.

Deforestation coupled with pressure on forests for various development purposes have caused decay of small-scale forest based industries in poor countries. The worst thing is that most of the cart manufacture industries become sick, non–viable to operate. Similarly, most of the wood based handicrafts industries have disappeared due to non-availability of wood. Because of strict regulation and declining of forest area the small entrepreneurs have started to use, secondary spiciness and non-wood forest product, for their survival.

The issue now is :

- how long the forest based small-scale industries can survive without raw materials ?
- what are the future prospects of these industries in India in the context of shrinking forest cover ?
- can substitute products for wood articles replace forest industries?
- how could additional employment be generated?
- is their any way to involve their small-scale industries for regenerating forests, so that they can get wood sustainably?

Global Warming, Green House Effects, and Ozone Layer Depletion

Studies have shown that the globe is getting warmer and warmer by two to six degree celsius in every 25 years. Six of the seven warmest years (out of last 150 years) occurred since 1980. Because of this reason tropical forests are disappearing and many of the tropical grasslands face the danger of being transformed to desert or temperate grasslands (Anon, 1998b: 1). Since the mean sea level is rising many islands will submerge into the sea. South Asia is the most vulnerable in absolute terms. Maldives, Bangladesh and Lakshadweep are few cases to notify. The climatic changes adversely affect agricultural production in developing countries and positively influence in the western cold countries, but the latter will be the greater sufferers of disease, which is not endemic now. Now, every one accept that human action are mostly responsible for global warming.

Burning of fossil fuels is the major culprit for the present problem of green house cases, CO_2, CFC, Methane, Nitrous oxide and other gases are major contributing factors for green house gases. A major portion of CO_2 is omitted from vehicles. Rice fields and cattles also produce major methene gas. Although the per capita emission of CO_2 in the world is only 1.2 tonnes, the Chinese (7 tonnes), Americans' (5 tonnes), and Canadians' (5 tonnes) produce more CO_2.

The increasing concentration of Chloro Fluora Carbon (CFC) in the atmosphere causes ozone layer depletion. The CFC is present in refrigerators, air conditioners, and aerosol. It is estimated that 15 million tonnes of CFC was expelled in to the atmosphere till 1987. A hole was noted in the ozone layer in Antarctica and the Northern Hemisphere. The depletion of ozone layer may lead to skin cancer, reduce the resistance power, reduce the power of photosynthesis in plants, reduce fish availability in sea and this may pave the way for acid rain.

The important issues are :

- how to contain the global warming ? when the advanced countries like USA has not willing to reduce CO_2 by the prescribed level of Kyoto protocol by 2010 how can poor countries co-operate with the treaty ?
- is there any way to reduce the concentration of CFC in the atmosphere ?
- are the people are willing to forgo the use of air-conditioners, refrigerators, and aerosol for the cause of clean atmosphere?
- what are the measures available with the small enterprises to reduce CO_2, NO, and CFC in the context of saving our fragile environment?

Conclusion

Small Industries are only a part of pollution creators. But the magnitude and type of waste disposals are much lesser than the amount of wastage and pollution emitted by the large scale industries. Comparing to the quantum of employment and its share to total employment generated by all types of industrial category, the damages caused by the small-scale industries on the environment is too little. Most of the environmental problems arise due to wrong usage of science and technology for advancement of human beings. However, it is our own responsibility to treat all environment-related problems as social problems and participate ourselves in solving these problems on war footing. It is the responsibility of the state to provide basic minimum needs to the people without harming the environment. The State should try to adopt a strategy of sustainable and eco-friendly development for all its future economic development. Similarly, the small entrepreneurs and all citizens should act in a responsible manner either extracting natural resources or using the output of these natural resources without harming the environment. Industries can motivate the public to plant more trees, not to use plastic bags, and re-cycle the products after use. In this way the industry can play as a key partner for sustainable development. Panchayat Presidents, Non-governmental organisations and self-help groups can actively participate in development programmes and create awareness among the people about safe drinking water, afforestation, better sanitation, and good health practices.

REFERENCES

Anon (1998a), *Valuing the Global Environment: Actions and Investments for the 21st Century*, Global Environmental Facility: 162.

Anon (1998b), *Climate Change, Report Prepared as Background for Buenos Aires Meeting of CCF*, Hadley Centre for Climate Prediction and Research.

Anon (2000a), *Global Environmental outlook,* United Nations Environment Programme: 12.

Anon (2000b), *Global Environmental Outlook*, United Nations Environmental Programme: 12.

Giles Atkinson, Richard Dubourg, Nirk Hamilton, Mohan Munasinghe, David Peace, and Carlose Young (1999), *Measuring Sustainable Development : Macroeconomics and the Environment,* Edward Elgar, Chelten Home, U.K. : 252.

Khan, Mohammad Shabbir (1994), *Current Problems of Indian Economy*, Ashia Publishing House, New Delhi. 262.

Narain, Sunita and Anil Agarwal (1996). 'Earth Summit – All Talk No Action', *The Hindu Survey of Environment*, 1996, 7-9.

Sankaran, S. (1994), *Environmental Economics*, Margo Publications, Madras : 434.

Schumacher, E.F (1993), *Small is Beautiful: A Study of Economics as if people mattered*, Vintage Publication, London, U.K.: 259.

Sudhir, M.A. (2001), 'Environmental Issues: An Approach Paper', *National Workshop on Environmental Issues*. April 27-28, 2001, Gandhigram Rural Institute, Gandhigram.

Varatharajan. S, and S. Elangovan (1992), *Environmental Economics*, A Speed Publications, Madurai, India: 246,

7

Capital Budgeting

P. ARUMUKHAM

Importance of Profit

Investment decisions are known as capital budgeting. A business makes investment in anticipation of an expected flow of benefits over a period of time. Therefore, when business has to choose from a number of initially exclusive investments decision will be determined by the amount of benefits. In micro economics maximisation of profits is the basis of the behaviour of business institutions. All actions in respect of size of output, cost and price are determined with the sole objective of maximising profit. Profit-maximisation, in short, is the criterion of economic efficiency in the perspective of economic theory. In the sphere of financial management also profitability of business operation has for long been a major financial goal.[1]

Conceptual Problems of Profit

However, efficacy of profitability as a measure of efficiency in financial management is questioned on two counts, viz., ambiguity in the concept of profit and implications of time element in the flow of profit.[2]

There are various concepts of profit like gross profit, profit before depreciation, profit after interest and profit after tax and choosing of any one of them will be difficult. The most significant objection to profit maximisation as a goal of financial management is that the time element that separates out flow of capital and inflow of profit. For instance an investment made in year t_0 may fetch profit in years t_1, t_2 and t_3. In relating profit in t_3 to investment into value of money in both t_0 and t_3 are assumed to be equal which is not true.

In view of the above objections, maximisation of wealth instead of maximisation of profit, is advocated as a goal of financial management[3]. However this new goal, as Prof. Hampton points out, places emphasis on profit only – though indirectly—since wealth of the business is gathered from the profit of the business[4]. Therefore, profitability has remained a very useful tool both for planning of investment and evaluation of financial management. All text books on financial management deal with profitability ratios as part of ratio analysis. However the concept of profit should be carefully chiseled in order to avoid any ambiguity. Anticipated profit is estimated in the form of cash flow during the life of the project. Also provision must be made for the time-interval that separates investment and profit with the help of an appropriate time-preference rate or discount-rate. This can be done either by compounding initial cash outflow, i.e., capital or by discounting subsequent cash inflow or profit.

Table 7.1 : Inflow of Cash

Years	*Inflow of Cash From*		
	Project-1	*Project-2*	*Project-3*
1.	32,000	32,000	40,000
2.	40,000	43,000	50,000
3.	43,000	52,000	60,000
4.	50,000	50,000	50,000
5.	50,000	40,000	30,000
6.	43,000	23,000	–
7.	15,000	–	–

Table 7.2 : Present Value of Inflow of Cash

Year	*Project-I*			*Project-II*		*Project-III*	
	Cash inflow Rs.	*PV.F. X*	*P.V. of Cash XX Rs.*	*Cash inflow Rs.*	*P.V. of Cash inflow Rs.*	*Cash inflow Rs.*	*P.V. of Cash inflow Rs.*
1	32,000	0.877	28,064	32,000	28,064	40,000	35,080
2	40,000	0.769	30,760	43,000	33,067	50,000	38,450
3	43,000	0.675	29,025	52,000	35,100	60,000	40,500
4	50,000	0.592	29,600	45,000	26,640	50,000	29,600
5	50,000	0.519	25,950	30,000	15,570	30,000	15,570
6	43,000	0.456	19,608	23,000	10,488	—	—
7	15,000	0.400	6,000	—	—	—	—
Total present value			1,69,007 or 1,69,000		1,48,929 or 1,48,900		1,59,200
Less investment			1,50,000		1,50,000		1,50,000
Net Present Value (NPV)			19,000		(-)1,100		9,200

A firm may evaluate three investment proposals of the following project each requiring an investment of Rs.1,50,000. The cost of capital to the firm is 14 per cent.

By dividing investment of Rs. 1,50,000/- by the average cash flow of Rs. 46,000 we get 3.261 which may be considered as an unity present value factor for 5 years; the life of all projects. The above factor of 3.261 is very near the P.A of 16 per cent (at 3.274) I.R.R. may lie between 14 per cent and 18 per cent.

CAPITAL BUDGETING : PROFITABILITY

I.R.R.

A project requiring an investment of Rs.1,50,000 is expected to generate cash inflow of Rs.40,000, Rs.50,000, Rs.60,000, Rs.50,000 and Rs.30,000 in five years. Calculate the I.R.R. of this project.

Average inflow of cash in project life amounts to

$$\frac{\text{Rs. } 40{,}000 + \text{Rs. } 50{,}000 + \text{Rs. } 60{,}000 + \text{Rs. } 50{,}000 + \text{Rs. } 30{,}000}{5}$$

= Rs. 2,30,000/5 = Rs.46,000.

Therefore, we should compute present value of cash flow using interest rates of 14 per cent, 16 per cent and 18 per cent. For calculating the present value of cash inflow present value factor for interest rates of 14 per cent, 16 per cent and 18 per cent may be taken from table on (present value of Re.1) for five years .

Table 7.3 : Internal Rate of Return

Year	*Cash*	*At 14%*		*At 16%*		*At 18%*	
		P.V.F.	*P.V.*	*P.V.F.*	*P.V.*	*P.V.F.*	*P.V.*
1	40,000	0.877	35,080	0.862	34,480	0.847	33,880
2	50,000	0.769	38,450	0.743	37,150	0.718	35,900
3	60,000	0.675	40,500	0.641	38,460	0.609	36,540
4	50,000	0.592	29,600	0.552	27,600	0.516	25,800
5	30,000	0.519	15,570	0.476	14,280	0.437	13,110
			1,59,200		1,51,970		1,45,230
Less Capital Outlay			1,50,000		1,50,000		1,50,000
Net present value			9,200		1,970		(-)4,770

From the above table it becomes clear that the actual I.R.R. should lie between 16 per cent and 18 per cent.

The actual I.R.R. can be approximated between 16 per cent and 18 per cent by interpolation using the following formula.

I.R.R = L + D1/D2 × Dr

Where L = Lower rate of interest

D1 = Difference between calculated present value of lower rate of interest and required cash flow.

D2 = Difference between the two calculated present values

Dr = Difference in rates

L + D1/D2 × Dr.

$$= 16 + \frac{151970 - 150000}{151970 - 145230} \times 2$$

$$= 16 + 1970/6740 \times 2 = 16 + 3940/6740$$

$$= 16 + 0.58 = 16.58 \text{ per cent}$$

Thus I.R.R. for the above project is 16.58 per cent.

REFERENCES

1. For instance Walker E.W. in his *Essentials of Financial Management*, Prentice Hall of India, New Delhi suggests only two methods for evaluating performance of business. They are (1) Return to Investment and (2) Fund Flow Statement, pp. 30-33.
2. Francis, P., *The Foundation of Financial Management*, Arnold-Heisemanu (1983), p. 20-21.
3. Horne, J.C.V., *op. cit.* p.7.
4. Hampton, J.J., *op. cit.* p.10.
5. Pandey, I.M. *Financial Management,* Vikas.

8

Working Capital : Operating Cycle

R. SEERANGARAJAN AND P. ARUMUKHAM

Importance of Working Capital

Working capital is a major area of managerial concern. A substantial part of management's time is devoted to routine operations of the business which can be subsumed under the heading working capital management[1]. Investment in working capital is both large and volatile calling for close and constant attention. Moreover investment in fixed capital can be avoided through renting and leasing whereas investment in working capital cannot be bye-passed, hence the importance of working capital.

Kind of Working Capital

There are two concepts of working capital viz. gross working capital and net working capital. Gross working capital, also simply called working capital, is the sum of current assets chiefly comprising cash, stocks in trade, debtors and other kinds of receivable. Net working capital is the surplus of current assets over current liabilities[2]. In other words net working capital is that part of the current asset which is financed with long term funds. While management may be more concerned with current assets (Gross Working Capital) for sustaining the tempo of production and marketing a bank is more interested in net working capital of the business, i.e. availability of long term funds for discharging short-term obligations. This study pursues management's view-point thus concentrating on gross working capital. In Management's perception current assets in themselves represent blocking of cash. Excess of current assets over current liabilities as represented by net working capital gives no particular comfort to management. What is more relevant to it than net working capital is the adequacy of current assets as well as their liquidity.

Operating Cycle

In manufacturing activity cash is needed to buy raw materials and store, pay wages and salaries and incur a number of other expenses. This out-flow of cash is recovered when sale-proceeds of finished goods are realised. The cash, thus recovered, is used again for purchase of raw materials etc., thus repeating the cycle. Cash in this cycle becomes raw materials, work in progress, goods in storage and sundry debtors before it becomes once again cash. "The continuing flow from cash to suppliers, inventories to amounts receivable and back into cash is what is called the operating cycle"[3].

The operating cycle consists of raw material cycle, conversion cycle, storange and collection cycle. Raw materials cycle consists of gross raw materials cycle and net raw material cycle. Duration gross raw materials cycle is the time spent by raw material in store awaiting conversion. Net raw material cycle is obtained through subtraction of duration of trade credit from the gross raw material cycle. Thus net raw material cycle is the time spent by cash in the time spent by cash in form of raw materials. In the event of cash purchase, gross raw material cycle and net raw material cycle will be equal.

Conversion cycle is the time spent by cash in the process of conversion. Time spent by cash in the form of finished foods in godown is storage cycle and duration of collection of debtors is collection cycle. These can be computed as shown below.

1. Gross raw material cycle $= \dfrac{\text{Average Stock of raw material r.m.}}{\text{Average daily rate of consumption of raw material}}$

2. Duration of trade credit $= \dfrac{\text{Average Sundry Creditors}}{\text{Daily Credit Purchase}}$

3. Net raw material cycle $= \dfrac{\text{Gross Raw Material}}{\text{Duration of trade credit}}$

4. Conversion cycle $= \dfrac{\text{Average Stock of Work in Progress}}{\text{Average cost of goods produced per day}}$

5. Storage cycle $= \dfrac{\text{Average Stock of finished goods}}{\text{Average cost of goods sold per day}}$

6. Collection Cycle $= \dfrac{\text{Average Sundry Debtors}}{\text{Average daily credit sales}}$

7. Operating Cycle = Net raw material cycle + conversion cycle + storage cycle + collection cycle
8. Turnover of working capital = 365/operating cycle

An illustration of operating cycle can be seen in the Appendix.

REFERENCES

1. Weston, J.F. and Brigham E.F., *Essentials of Managerial Finance*, The Doyden Press Hinsdale, Illinois (Ved) p.173.
2. Gitman, L.J., *Principles of Managerial Finance*, Harper & Row, New York (1976), p.150.
3. Smit, K.V., *Management of Working Capital*, West Publishers (1974) p.7
4. Chakraborthy, S.K., Bhattacharya, K.K., Rao N.K and Sen, P.K, *Financial Management and Control,* Macmillan India Ltd., New Delhi.
5. Sandilya, M.S. and Gopalakrishnan, P., *Inventory Management Text & Cases,* Macmillan India Ltd., New Delhi.

Appendix : Chenkumar Society, Chennimalai Operating Cycle

Furnishing Category – Large (Rs. in lakhs)

S. No	Particulars	*1988–89*	*1989–90*	*1990–91*	*1991–92*	*1992–93*	*1993–94*	*1994–95*	*1995–96*	*1996–97*	*1997–98*	*1998–99*
I. Raw Material Cycle												
1	Op. Stock of raw materials	6.92	12.98	31.90	21.69	22.78	24.74	20.48	42.77	67.84	67.84	42.52
2	Purchase of raw materials	221.69	232.53	268.68	358.51	377.85	374.31	491.31	508.1	415.2	488	504.6
3	Total (1+2)	228.61	245.51	300.58	380.2	400.63	399.05	511.79	550.87	483.04	455.84	567.12
4	(–) Closing stock of raw materials	12.98	30.9	21.69	22.78	24.77	20.48	42.77	67.84	67.84	62.52	39.68
5	Raw material transacted (3–4)	215.63	214.61	278.89	357.42	375.86	378.57	469.02	483.03	415.2	493.32	527.44
6	Value of raw materials consumed	215.63	213.61	278.89	357.42	375.86	378.57	469.02	483.03	415.2	493.32	527.44
7	Average of transaction of raw materials per day (5/365)	0.6	0.59	0.77	0.98	1.03	1.04	1.09	1.32	1.14	1.35	1.44
8	Average stock of raw materials (1+4)/2	9.95	21.94	26.8	22.24	23.78	22.61	31.63	55.31	67.84	65.18	41.1
9	Gross raw materials cycle in days (8/7)	17.	38	35	23	24	22	25	60	59	48	29
10	Total purchase	221.69	232.53	268.68	358.51	377.85	374.31	491.31	508.1	415.2	488	504.6
11	Average daily purchase (10/365)	0.61	0.64	0.74	0.99	1.04	1.03	1.13	1.4	1.14	1.34	1.39
12	Average sundry creditors	12.24	20.02	9.12	10.44	6.55	6.76	14.48	9.36	14.39	20.66	78.97
13	Duration of trade credit (12/11)	20	31	12	11	6	7	13	7	13	15	37
14	Net raw material cycle (9–13) in days	– 3	8	23	12	17	16	16	35	46	33	–22
II. Conversion Cycle												
15	Opening stock of work-in-progress	17.1	19.81	24.23	32.57	47.9	33.38	37	50.54	33.25	49.9	57.32
16	Purchase of work-in-progress	–	–	–	–	–	–	–	–	–	–	–
17	Raw materials consumed (vide–I.6)	215.63	213.61	278.89	357.42	375.86	378.6	397.02	483.03	415.2	493.32	527.44
18	Manufacturing cost	127.51	145.93	160.76	187.84	238.91	258.88	291.15	328.78	381	465.45	519.61
19	Total (15+16+17+18)	360.24	379.35	463.88	577.83	662.67	670.86	725.17	862.35	829.45	1008.67	1104.37
20	Closing stock of work-in-progress	19.81	24.23	32.57	47.9	33.38	37	50.54	33.25	49.9	57.32	64.24
21	Cost of finished goods manufactured (19–20)	340.43	355.12	431.31	529.39	629.29	633.86	674.63	829.1	779.55	951.35	1040.13
22	Total value of transaction	340.43	355.12	431.31	529.39	629.29	633.86	674.63	829.1	779.55	951.35	1040.13
23	Average value of transaction per day (22/365)	0.932	0.973	1.183	1.45	1.72	1.74	1.85	2.27	2.14	2.61	2.85

Contd.

S. No	Particulars	1988–89	1989–90	1990–91	1991–92	1992–93	1993–94	1994–95	1995–96	1996–97	1997–98	1998–99
24	Average stock of work–in–progress (15+20)/2	18.46	22.02	28.4	40.23	40.64	35.19	43.77	41.89	41.57	53.61	60.78
25	Average duration of conversion cycle	20	23	24	28	24	20	24	18	19	20	21
III.	**Storage Cycle**											
26	Op. Stock of finished goods	92.37	87.56	90.5	68.1	93.2	82.29	60.8	58.47	132.5	173.72	212.43
27	Purchase of finished goods	–	–	–	–	–	–	–	–	–	–	–
28	Cost of finished goods manufactured (II.21)	340.43	355.12	431.31	529.93	629.29	633.86	674.63	829.1	779.55	951.35	1040.13
29	Total (26 + 27 + 28)	432.8	442.77	521.81	598.03	722.49	716.15	735.43	887.57	912.05	1125.07	1252.56
30	Closing stock	87.65	90.5	68.1	93.2	82.29	60.8	58.47	132.5	173.72	212.43	195.2
31	Cost of Goods produced (29–30)	345.15	352.27	453.71	504.83	640.2	655.35	676.96	755.07	738.33	912.64	1057.36
32	Distribution expenses (Packing, forwarding, transport and sales commission)	–	–	–	–	–	–	–	–	–	–	–
33	Cost of goods sold (31–32)	345.15	352.27	453.71	504.83	640.2	655.35	676.96	755.07	738.33	912.64	1057.36
34	Average cost of goods sold per day (33/365)	0.95	0.96	1.24	1.38	1.75	1.79	1.85	2.07	2.02	2.50	2.89
35	Average stock of finished goods (26+30)/2	90.01	89.07	79.3	80.65	87.74	71.54	59.63	95.48	153.11	386.15	203.81
36	Storage cycle (35/34) in days	95	93	64	58	50	40	32	46	76	154	70
IV.	**Collection Cycle**											
37	Total Credit Sales	217.8	230	290	257	412	336	487	510.6	602.5	707.2	740.6
38	Average daily credit sales (37/365)	0.59	0.63	0.79	0.78	1.13	0.92	1.33	1.39	1.65	1.94	2.03
39	Average sundry debtors	180.55	187.18	206.77	200.94	243.61	234.43	300.4	377.86	400.3	405.02	521.5
40	Duration of collection cycle–in– days (39/38)	302	297	262	254	216	255	226	272	243	209	254
V.	**Total Operating Cycle**											
41	Net raw materials cycle in days	–3	8	23	12	17	16	16	35	46	33	– 22
42	Conversion cycle in days	20	23	24	28	24	20	24	18	19	20	21
43	Storage cycle in days	95	93	64	58	50	40	32	46	76	154	70
44	Collection cycle in days	302	297	262	254	216	255	226	272	243	209	254
45	Total cycle days	414	421	373	352	307	331	298	371	384	416	326
46	Turnover of working capital (365/45)	0.88	0.86	0.98	1.03	1.18	1.1	1.23	0.98	0.95	0.88	1.12

Note: Items 2, 4, 12, 15, 16, 18 and 20 are the basic data drawn from books of accounts.
Source: Audited Statement of Annual Accounts of Chenkumari Society.

9

Communication in Organizations

OOMMEN MATHEW

Organizations, large and small, commercial and not-for-profit, religious and educational—are all structured to facilitate the achievement of objectives. The communication process in an organization connects superiors, subordinates, members of the peer group and the external environment. The top man's job is almost solely communication as he has the main task of linking and relating the organization with the environment.

In the absence of communication, human beings will have to exist as individuals never benefiting from the sharing of emotions, experiences, knowledge etc. Without communication, which has undisputed primary in the affairs of human race, man will not be able to unite to overcome limitations and ensure achievements.

Communication involves the transfer or rather exchange of ideas, information, understanding, feelings emotions etc. between individuals. It can be defined as *"who says what and why to whom through which channel with what effect"*. Though this is a reasonably comprehensive definition of communication, it is a process oriented one. It should be stated in this context that the concept of communication is *Common Understanding* between the involved parties—whom we shall refer to as the *Sender* and *Receiver* – about what is being communicated which we shall term as *Message*. "Message" may denote anything ranging from ideas to data to statistics to emotions and feelings.

The Importance of Communication

Studies have been conducted on the amount of time spent on communication by people from different walks of life. It is found that the group that has to spend least time for the process of communication is the shop floor level workers in manufacturing organizations. Even in their case, 40 to 60 per cent of time is spent on communication. As a person's position in the organizational echelon is higher and higher, the time required to be spent on communication is more and more. The head of any organization may be expected to spend more than 80 per cent of his/her time on some form of communication or the other. What this means is that how effectively, efficiently, creatively and productively that person communicates will decide his overall effectiveness, efficiently, creativity and productivity to a corresponding extent. The communication process in any organization is so vital for the achievement of its objectives. How a communication system is managed in an organization, i.e. how effective it is, has a profound impact on the ultimate effectiveness of the total organization.

Numerous studies have confirmed the impact of communication organizational productivity efficiency and effectiveness. In one such study, the reasons for wide variations in productivity among twenty seven branches of a package-delivery organization, were explored. As part of the study communication data were collected from the 975 employees from the branches. Comparison of productivity and communication data revealed positive correlation between high performance and open communication between superiors and subordinates.[1]

In a survey conducted among nearly a hundred business organizations with the objective of determining how much of what top management has to say is actually understood, the following facts were revealed.[2]

(1) At the Vice-Presidential level managers understand about two thirds of what they hear from the top.
(2) At the general supervisor level managers understand 56 per cent of the top-level information.
(3) At the manager level managers perceive only 40 per cent.
(4) Foremen perceive 30 per cent.
(5) Persons on the production line understand 20 per cent.

The above findings throw light on the need and potential for management by bettering improving communication skills.

The ABCs of Communication

Like any other process, communication also has its ABCs and it is interesting to note that the ABCs of communication are:

A – Attractiveness
B – Brevity
C – Clarity

The Process of Communication

Whatever is being communicated is called *'Message'*. The person from whom the message originates—the one who initiates the process of communication—is called the *Sender.* The person for whom the communication is meant is called the *Receiver* Communication cannot take place in a vacuum. It has to have a medium or channel. After receiving the message the 'Receiver' will react or respond to the sender when provision for that exists. This part of the communication process may be termed *'Feedback'*. When there is no provision for *'Receiver to Sender Feedback'*, it may be called one-way communication. This, in most cases, may increase the distortion between the intended message and the one that is received. There are various barriers to effective communication which may affect the process at any stage and they can be collectively designated by the term 'NOISE'. The following model will illustrate the process of communication.

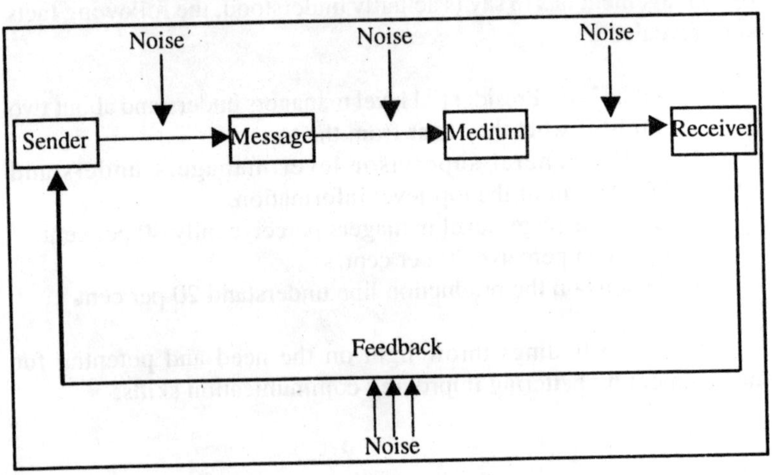

Communication Categories

Based on the presence or absence of two important attributes of communication viz., effectiveness and impressiveness, all communication can be grouped into one of the following categories:

— Effective and Impressive
— Effective but Unimpressive
— Ineffective but Impressive
— Ineffective and Unimpressive

Needless to mention, the best of the above lot is the first category and the last one is the worst. (It should be one's aim to make his/her communication effective and impressive). In the second and third categories, one attribute each is present while the other is lacking. If a choice is to be made between the second and third categories, definitely the preference must be for the second one. In other words, if we have to prioritise, effectiveness has primacy.

Barriers to Effective Organizational Communication

There are many barriers that can impede the process of communication resulting in a communication breakdown. Some of the common barriers to effective communication are described below. However, it should be remembered that the list is not exhaustive.

(i) *Transmission Alterations :* This refers to the changes that the original message undergoes when it passes through various people. The greater the differences between the people involved with respect to various factors like cultural background, social class, educational level, age group, experience etc. the greater will be the alterations that the message undergoes. One effective way to overcome the barrier—or at least reduce its ill effects—would be to ask the receiver to repeat what he/she has understood. This will provide the sender with an opportunity to make corrections to the perceived message if found necessary. When one has the role of the receiver and if the sender is not making any effort on the lines suggested above, the receiver may take the initiative for making the required clarifications.

(ii) Physical Limitations : The difference between perception and reality may be termed perceptual error. Our sensory limitations—those of sight, sound, touch, taste and smell—restrict perceptual clarity.

(iii) In attention : This is related to the receiver. When one has the role of the receiver, care should be taken to give proper attention to the message. When in sender's role, one should start communicating only after ensuring required level of attention on the part of the receivers. Despite physical proximity with the sender, the receiver's level of attention may come down or his/her thoughts may take side excursions while the sender is talking. The sender should recognize this as a natural and normal phenomenon and make efforts to regain receivers' attention at periodic intervals.

(iv) Selective Listening : When receivers tend to *"block out"* information, especially when it is contradictory to what one believes, it results in selective perception. It is a common practice for people to ignore or distort information that conflicts with ones prescribed notions.

(v) Mistrust of the Source : Over a period of time, we develop various levels of trust, confidence or faith in the words of the sender. It may be termed source credibility. To be an effective communicator, one should develop himself/herself as a credible source of information.

(vi) Exaggeration : People may resort to exaggeration to dramatize ones presentation or to make it more attractive, humorous etc. However, in the long run, one who is known to exaggerate always looses credibility.

(vii) Distortion : Distortion of the original message may occur due to various factors. Distortion may be accidental or intentional. In either case, the end result is undesirable and harmful.

(viii) Uniqueness : No two phenomena, no two things, no two human beings are exactly alike. Because of the uniqueness of individuals, their experiences, and as a result of this, their perceptions differ.

(ix) Badly Expressed Messages : Badly expressed messages may be the result of inadequate preparation, inadequate control over the medium, mannerisms of the sender etc. Even a wrong punctuation can result in badly expressed messages which may not convey any meaning or may convey an unintended message.

(x) Unclarified Assumptions : When one hears, sees or reads something he/she may make certain assumptions, which have no relation with reality. When one makes decisions or takes action based on wrong assumptions, the result will be disastrous.

(xi) Abstractions : In abstracting—the process of leaving something out to derive meaning—people give differential emphasis

to different factors. Because of this, different people, when bombarded with the same stimulus or set of stimuli, may give different responses based on different conclusions.

(xii) Absentmindedness : Mental pre-occupation resulting in absentmindedness can be a very important barrier to effective communication. When in the role of the receiver, one should safeguard himself/herself from it and when in the sender's role, should watch for signs of absentmindedness on the part of the receiver and take steps to ensure proper attention and involvement.

(xiii) Time Pressure : People in positions of authority and responsibility may not have enough time to communicate with everybody. Time pressure can result in improper and insufficient communication. Time pressure may even lead to *short circuiting* which means people being left out of the formal channel of communication, who normally would have been included.

Improving Communication Skills

Remember the old adage, "Reading maketh a full man, writing an exacth man and conference a readyman" and practice it to be a wise communicator.

Though there are various forms of communication, more often than not, we communicate orally. Oral communication involves :

(i) Listening
(ii) Speaking

To get an idea of how good ones listening is one may give 'yes' or 'no' answers to the following questions :

(1) Are you waiting impatiently for the other fellow to shut up so that you can talk?
(2) Are you in such a hurry to offer a solution that you don't want to hear the problem?
(3) Are you listening only for what you like to hear?
(4) Do emotional blocs get in the way of your listening?
(5) Do your prejudices interfere with your listening?
(6) Do your thoughts take side excursions while the other fellow is talking?

(7) Are you memorizing more details instead of getting the main points ?
(8) Do you quit listening when the subject matter gets difficult ?
(9) Do you have a negative attitude while listening?
(10) Do you just pretend to listen?
(11) Do you put yourself in the speakers place to understand what makes him say that?
(12) Do you take into account that you and the speaker may not be discussing the same question?
(13) Are you alert for misunderstanding that could arise because the words don't mean the same to you as they do to the speaker?
(14) Do you try to find out what the argument is about? Whether there is a real difference of opinions or is it just a matter of stating the problem?

The ideal answers for each of the questions from 1 to 10, *No* and for 11 to 14, *Yes.*

To evaluate oneself as a speaker, the following thirteen questions may be answered *Yes* or *No.*

(1) Are you careful to watch for signs of misunderstandings in your listener?
(2) Do you choose words that fit the listener's intelligence and backgrounds?
(3) Do you think out directions before giving them?
(4) Do you breakdown orders into small enough packages?
(5) If a subordinate does not ask questions about a new idea you are presenting, do you assume that he understands it?
(6) Do you speak distinctly? Control distractions as far as possible?
(7) Do you 'bale' your thoughts before speaking so that you won't ramble?
(8) Do you put the listener at ease?
(9) Do you encourage questions?
(10) (a) Do you assume that you know what the other fellow has in his mind?
(b) Or do you ask questions to find out?
(11) Do you distinguish between facts and opinions?

(12) Do you stiffen up the opposition by contradicting his/her/ their statements?
(13) Do you influence your subordinates to be "Yes Sir" or "Yes Madam" people?

Ideal answers for the above questions would be as follows:

Question Nos.	*Ideal Answer*
1 to 4	Yes
5	No
6 to 9	Yes
10 (a)	No
10 (b) and 11	Yes
12 and 13	No

Improving Presentation Skills

Irrespective of whether ones social and/or organizational roles require him/her to address mammoth gatherings, medium sized crowds or just small groups, presentation skills have a significant role in determining ones overall effectiveness and efficiency. The ability to make good presentations is a skill that one acquires, at least mainly, through practice.

On page 108 is given a Rating Scale for Assessing Performance of presentations. This was developed but the author for use in long term training programmes where each participant will be given a few opportunities to make presentations. When one is making a presentation, all the other members of the batch—who will constitute the audience—will be given a copy of the rating scale. The members of the audience will write the name of the trainee at the space provided for the same and will indicate their opinions of the presentation with respect to various attributes. The use of the rating scale enables objective and systematic peer-group feedback as the observers are forced to comment on various attributes rather than making too generalized statements. After the presentation is over and the rating scales completed by the observers, they are handed over to the person who made the presentation. This enables him/her to make a consolidated feed back report which can be used for personal development. Feedback reports thus obtained over a period of time can be compared to get an idea of the progress the trainee is making.

SLSD* OM *SLED*

Table 9.1 : Rating Scale for Assessing Performance of Presentations

Name of Trainee:

Sl. No	*Attribute*	*Rating*				
		Excellent	*Good*	*So So*	*Poor*	*Bad*
1.	Correctness of Language	–	–	–	–	–
2.	Clarity of words	–	–	–	–	–
3.	Clarity of thought	–	–	–	–	–
4.	Logical sequence of ideas	–	–	–	–	–
5.	Speed	–	–	–	–	–
6.	Audibility	–	–	–	–	–
7.	Voice Modulation	–	–	–	–	–
8.	Use of pauses	–	–	–	–	–
9.	Body posture	–	–	–	–	–
10.	Facial Expression	–	–	–	–	–
11.	Eye contact with audience	–	–	–	–	–
12.	Gestures	–	–	–	–	–
13.	Mannerisms (visual and vocal)	–	–	–	–	–
14.	Confidence	–	–	–	–	–
15.	Overall impression	–	–	–	–	–

* SLSD – Social Lab for Self Development and SLED.S.Lab FOR executive Development are two training packages developed by the author, in which this rating scale, devised by him, is used.

Improving Organizational Communication

There is no magic formula for ensuring effective organizational communication as it is too complicated a process. However, organizational communication can be bettered. An awareness of the barriers to effective communication will help in two ways: (1) avoiding the barriers or reducing their ill effects in one's communicaton (2) anticipating communication malfunctions in others which helps to overcome many a barrier in communication.

In ones effort to become a better communicator, he/she must not only strive to be understood but also to understand. The task is two fold. First, the message must be improved. So should be the understanding of what other people are trying to communicate to them. Some techniques that will aid in the accomplishment of these tasks are discussed below:

1. Receiver Orientation : To improve communication, one should speak the language of the receiver. Care should be taken to use words and usages that suit the listeners intelligence and background.

2. Attention to the ABCs : As a guiding principle for effective communication it should always be remembered to give proper attention to the ABCs viz. attractiveness, brevity and clarity.

3. Appropriateness : Appropriateness in communication means a lot of things. There should not be too much or too little of communication. It should not be too formal or too informal. It should sound serious or humourous depending on the topic being discussed, the nature of the receiver, time availability etc.

4. Use of Humour : Communication process is akin to the functioning of a machinery with moving parts which requires lubrication for smooth friction-free operation. An effective 'lubricant' for the process of communication is humour. However, care should be taken to use it judiciously to avoid unintended or negative results.

5. Use of Right Appeal : The effectiveness of communication will be greatly enhanced when the right appeal is used. The skill of the communicator lies in identifying the right appeal for each situation and then using it.

6. Repetition : The universally acknowledged principle of learning viz. repetition can greatly contribute to communication effectiveness. Repetition will ensure that even if one part of the message is not understood, there are other parts which will carry the same meaning.

7. Effective Timing : A host of messages compete for peoples attention simultaneously. Many are not even decoded or received just because of the impossibility of taking them all in. Messages are best understood and received when they face least competition from other messages. Improper timing can result in distortions and value judgments which are harmful.

8. Simplifying Language : Many people, especially teachers and trainers have the habit of resorting to technical jargon that transforms simple concepts into complex puzzles. Complicated language is a very important barrier to effective communication. It has to be recognized that effective communication involves transmitting *understanding* as well as information

9. Effective Listening : Effective listening is as important to communication as effective speaking. Managers must not only seek to be understood but also to *understand.* By proper listening, one can encourage others to express true feelings, hopes, aspirations and emotions. More than just listening, *listening with understanding* is what is required.

Guidelines for Improving Communication

The following may be thought of as Ten Commandments of Effective Communication.

I. Be sure of what you wish to communicate and why

Be sure of your objective in communicating:

* Do you want further information?
* Do you wish to initiate a certain type of action?
* Do you wish to change the behaviour of your receiver?

II. Use language with clarity

* Use the receiver's language
* Your objective is not to chock or over-power the receiver

III. Watch how much you communicate

* Not too much to cause boredom
* Not too little, as that may not remove the communication gap

IV. Use adequate medium

* Select oral, written or visual medium as you consider most effective

V. Provide the right climate

* Select the right physical setting
* Remove organizational blocks or,

reduce their effect by being conscious of their existence.

VI. Listen attentively

* Avoid marginal listening
* Induce projective listening
* Develop the skill of empathic listening.

VII. Watch out unintentional communications

* Watch carefully the tone of your voice
* Avoid the frown, the bored look and fidgeting.

VIII. Remember communication is a two way process

* Be sure the message is perceived correctly

IX. Practice what you preach. Action speak louder than words

X. Provide communication training. Improve the oral and written communications – encourage effective speaking, listening and report writing.

Conclusion

The above discussion attempted to convey the basics in the process of communication and means and techniques for effective communication. The principles described apply to oral and written communication and is equally significant whether communication is vertical, horizontal or diagonal. Some of the techniques suggested for improving communication may find difficulty in being translated into action for want of time. However, it is hoped that the discussion has thrown enough light on the challenge of effective communication and its requirements. Managers have to be effective in both transmission and reception. They must communicate effectively in their endeavour to understand and be understood, which will go a long way in improving their effectiveness and efficiency as managers.

REFERENCES

1. Haney, Willaim V: Communication and Organizational Behaviour, Irwin, Homewood, III, 1973.
2. Lesikar, Raymond V: Business Communication: Theory and Application, Irwin, Homewood, III, 1972.
3. Douglas G Curley, The Other Half of Employee Communication, The Personnel Administration, July 1979, p. 29.
4. George de Mare, Communicating at the Top, John Wiley & Sons, New York, 1979.
5. Baron, Alma S. "Communication Skills for the Woman Manager – A Practice Seminar", Personnel Journal, Jan. 1980
6. Gary L. Benson, "On the Campus: How well do Business Schools Prepare Graduates for the Business World"? Personnel, July-August 1983, pp.63-65
7. Shapiro, Irvings, "Executive Forum: Managerial Communication: The View from Inside", California Management, Fall, 1984. p.157.

* Bernard P. Indik, Basil S. Georgopoulos and Stanley E. Seashore, "Superior-Subordinate Relationship and Performance", *Personal Psychology,* Winter, 1961, p. 357-374.

** "Understand What you hear", *Nations Business* , Vol. 49, No.10, Oct. 1961, p. 94

10

Renewable Energy Technologies for Rural Industries

S. RAMASWAMY AND P. KANNIAPPAN

Introduction

Energy has always been a factor of fundamental importance in the life of human societies. Throughout the history of mankind, major advances in civilization have been accompanied by an increased use of energy. Present day civilization and culture, as well as day to day comforts, transport system, technology etc. all revolve around the energy we get from different sources. The food we eat, the fruits we consume, the water we drink, all have energy and by eating and drinking, we get energy to do our daily work and carry on our human existence. Thus, energy has been recognized as one of the most important inputs for national development. If, for example, our country has to achieve 8.0 per cent growth rate in the economy, then it would need commensurate inputs of different energy sources; most of these will be in the form of fossil fuels, and electricity. Energy economists also trace a correlation between the standard of living and energy use. According to the World Development Report 2001-2002, India has second largest population (1030 million) and one of the lowest per capita income ($ 450) and the lowest per capita consumption of energy (479 kilogram of oil equivalent). Moreover, per capita consumption of energy in India was just 5.9 per cent of the United States and 11.7 per cent of Japan. To increase the per capita energy consumption, more energy must be made available to our population for which two options are available to us. The first option is to explore the existing, recoverable fossil fuel resources, which are limited in nature and not eco-friendly. The second option is to make use of locally available non-conventional and renewable energy sources. The second option is highly suitable to Indian conditions because, India is endowed with large quantity of renewable energy resources.

Renewable Energy for Sustainable Development

Renewable energy sources and renewable energy technologies bring sustainable development. Sustainable development refers to responsible stewardship and development of earth's resources that permit future generations to enjoy atleast the present standard of living. Sustainable energy development is key to fighting poverty and hunger, enhancing health and social services, increasing productivity and income. Any shift from dependence on fossil fuels to increasing use of renewable sources of energy would be driven by changing the economic, social, political, cultural technological, environmental framework for equity and justice, economic parameters such as costs, investments, demand, supply and subsidies and lastly technological development to suit users needs.

Disparity in energy consumption is also found in between rural and urban areas of Indian economy. For instance 80.0 per cent of total energy consumed by 30.0 per cent urban population and 20.0 per cent of energy consumed by 70.0 per cent of rural population. To remove this 'energy inequality' it is the responsibility of the planners and scientists to make an efforts for increasing the energy supply through effective exploitation and utilization of non-conventional energy sources.

With this background, the authors of this paper have made an attempt to present the relevance of renewable energy and renewable energy technologies for rural development in general and sustainable rural development in particular by citing examples from selected rural industries.

With the depletion and hiking prices of fossil fuels, diesel and gas, the Indian economy is slowing down its growth rate. The impact is felt more in rural areas than in urban areas. The agricultural activities in rural India need more of these fuels for land preparation using tractors, water pumping and transportation of produces. Since the market prices of these produces stay stable, the rising production cost of agricultural products reduce the marginal profit, making the rural agricultural activities uneconomical and unpopular. This trend is harmful for an agricultural country like India. This trend is to be reversed to uplift the rural economy. The best method for uplifting the rural economy, is the adaptation of renewable energy technologies for selected rural industries. Today, the economic activities of the rural areas is highly depending upon both agricultural and selected small scale, cottage and village industries. The farmers could enhance their income when they get involved in both of these activities. After in-depth survey made in different villages in Tamil Nadu the authors present their experiences and suggestions for the development of rural industries which could benefit from renewable energy technologies. These industries are:

(1) Horticultural fruit and herbal plant farms;
(2) Silk reeling from cocoon industries;
(3) Wax-candle manufacturing industries;
(4) Herbal leaves drying industries;
(5) Waste materials briquetting industries;
(6) Dyeing Industries; and
(7) Emergency lighting through SPV Lantern.

Horticultural Fruits and Herbal Plant Farms

Under wasteland development scheme, rainfed waste lands can be converted into horticultural farms. Many horticultural crops, especially popular fruits yielding saplings are planted in some of the villages. These saplings are to be watered frequently till they can withstand different agro climatic variations. Most of these farms are away from common electric grid and thus there is no scope for electric pump sets. In such places, Solar Photo-Voltaic (SPV) pumping system is found to be very useful. If SPV is combined with drip irrigation system, the cost of watering is less. Besides the drip-irrigation system economizes the water need by five folds. For instance, two farms near the city of Madurai run profitability. The photo-voltaic system, bought through bank loan with low interest, could be cleared in four years. The fruit trees like guava, sappotta, custard apple etc bear fruits from third year onwards. The drip irrigation also minimizes the cost of human labour. The inter space (space between two plants) in the farm could be used for cultivation of herbal plants which will bring additional income to farm households. In wind potential area, mechanical windmills can be installed for water pumping. The PV water pumping system is trouble free and needs little maintenance. The popularization of hybrid PV pumping drip irrigation system will enhance the income of the rural farmers and generate additional employment opportunities.

Cocoon-Silk Reeling Industries

The authors of this paper had conducted a series of surveys in the villages around Theni town, and found that women are involved in cocoons silk reeling industries. Generally, silk cocoons are procured from weekly markets. These cocoons will yield silk yarn after the cocoons are degummed in hot water at 60°C. Women are using firewood and other bio fuels to prepare hot water for degumming. A small unit, employing 5 women, normally use about Rs.50.00 worth of firewood every day for preparation of hot water. In one cocoon silk reeling unit a solar flat-plate collector was installed at a total cost of Rs.10,000. The hot water from solar flat-plate collector was used for degumming the cocoon. Women can easily use this system in cocoon silk reeling unit. The quality of output from this unit remains the same. By adopting this technology, it is possible to save Rs.1000.00 worth of firewood per month. The estimated payback period is less than one year. This kind of technology could be popularized and propagated to these industries, which need hot water for carrying out their production process.

Wax-Candle Manufacturing Units

This industry generally uses kerosene based wick-stove for melting solid wax. Instead of using kerosene for melting solid wax, wax candle manufacturing unit can use solar cooker which cost Rs.2,500.00 per piece. A 50 cm × 50 cm solar cooker can melt 2kg of solid wax. If the vessel containing solid wax is placed in a solar cooker under good sunlight, the molten wax is ready in 30 minutes. The molten wax could be transferred to the modelling system. The final output namely, candle seems to be very clean and in proper shape. The estimated pay back period for this project is less than six months. Wax candle manufacturing unit could be managed by a woman. Self Help Groups can enter into this venture, which generates additional employment and income.

Herbal Leaves Drying Units

The demand for natural medicine produced with herbal has been continuously increasing in the regional, national and international markets. This situation has induced the farming communities to cultivate herbal plants in their land on commercial basis. Besides, many herbal gardens are coming up in different villages, particularly in hilly regions. Scientifically, these herbal leaves are to be properly dried before despatching to the processing centers. Some herbal leaves are heat sensitive and they are to be dried at appropriate temperature. The dried herbal products could be stored for longer period and then processed into herbal medicines. The herbal leaves drying units can use solar cabinet dryer for drying the herbal leaves. Solar energy experts opined that the solar cabinet dryer can be easily fabricated and maintained at low cost. For example, cardamom drying units have already started using the solar dryers which produce a good results and thus, this technology has been accepted by the cardamom planters. The solar dryers are being tried not in hilly villages.

Briquetting Industry

Villages in India possess a large quantity of agricultural wastes which are not properly used. The agricultural waste such as rice husk, saw dust, coir pith, groundnut shell, paddy straw, cotton stalks, etc are available in plenty in different seasons. These wastes are renewable sources of energy. The paddy straws, cotton plants, coconut pith etc are ignitable materials. These materials are in powdery forms or less dense in nature making it unsuitable for efficient burning. In order to make these fuel as efficient, they must be compressed into hard and dense material, for which briquetter — a mechanical device can be used. This device can compress the waste biomass into an efficient fuel. By doing so, the waste materials available in the Indian villages can be converted into a marketable product. The hard briquetted rod could substitute the firewood. The larger briquetter machines are available in the market. Big industrial units can adopt this technique and use briquetted rod as fuel in their production process.

Biomass can also be used for generating power through biomass based power projects, for which technically feasible and economically viable gasifier is now commercially available in the market. The gasifier produces 'producer gas' which could substitute 90 per cent of the fuel needs of diesel engines. These engines could produce electrical energy. The unelectrified remote villages could be electrified through biomass based power project. This process will generate employment opportunities in rural as well as villages which are located in the hilly regions. The authors had conducted a host of biomass assessment studies and estimated surplus biomass potential in various talukas of Tamil Nadu. The Ministry of Non-conventional Energy Sources (MNES) and Tamilnadu Energy Development Agency (TEDA) had done an impressive leadership in this matter. The results of these studies indicate that many talukas have potential to setup biomass based power projects, which can generate electrical energy and supply this energy to different villages. This project will make the villages as 'Energy Independent' and 'Energy Self-sufficient' and thus help to improve the living conditions of rural economy.

Dyeing Industrial Units

Dyeing industrial units are providing direct and indirect employment opportunities both in the rural and urban areas. These industries use a large quantity of firewood in their burners and the efficiency of the burners seem to be quiet low. If these industries use energy efficient gasifier in these units, a large quantity of firewood could be saved. By doing so, the problems of deforestation can be considerably reduced. For installation of gasifier, MNES is providing long term finance through nationalized commercial banks and IREDA.

Emergency Lighting Through SPV Lantern

There are about 80,000 villages in the country, which are still to be electrified. Of these, 18,000 villages are in remote and difficult areas such as hills, forests, deserts and island, which cannot be electrified by the conventional grid. Besides, many villages even after electrification do not get electric supply into their homes. Home lighting plays a significant role in improving the standard of living and literacy among the rural masses. The solar PV lanterns are presently available at subsidized rate, could play an impressive role in rural educational process and village industrial activities. A survey on 'SPV lantern and SPV street light users' has revealed a fact that the children perform well in their classes and women do some village handicraft manufacturing activities during night also. A prime example of demonstration of electrification through non-conventional energy in Sagar island in the Sundarbans region in West Bengal is note worthy.

Government Initiatives for Renewable Energy Technology

It is now recognized that renewable energy sources can provide the basis for sustainable energy development on account of their inexhaustible nature, and environment friendly features. Located in the tropical region, India is endowed with abundant natural resources (i.e., solar, wind, biomass including agricultural residues) which are perennial in nature. Harnessing these resources is best suitable to meet the energy requirements of rural areas, particularly rural industries and villages situated in difficult terrain. During the last two decades, several renewable energy technologies have been developed and deployed in the country. The major achievements along with the estimated potential in the areas of biomass and solar energy technologies are given below:

Table 10.1 : Renewable Energy potential and achievement as on 28.02.2002

Sources/System	*Approximate Potential*	*Achievement*
Biomass power	19500*	381MW
Biomass Gasifier		50MW
Solar Photo Voltaic	20MW/Sq. Km	
Solar Street Lighting System		41403 Nos.
Home lighting system		176962 Nos.
Solar Lanterns		382529 Nos.
SPV power plants		1172 Kwp
Solar water heating system	30 million sq. m collected area	590000 sq. m collected area
Solar cooking system		
Box type solar cookers		515000 Nos.
Concentrating type community cookers		175 Nos.
Solar PV pumps		4204 Nos.
Solar photo voltaic power		2.00 MW
Aditya solar shops		29 Nos.

* Including Biomass gasifier

In order to propagate renewable technologies, the Government of India has been taking serious efforts for harnessing the renewable energy sources for which the following programmes have been effectively implemented by the MNES:

- Solar Thermal Energy Programmes;
- Solar Cooker Programme;
- Solar Photovoltaic Programme;
- SPV Water Pumping Programme;
- National Project on Biogas Development;
- Community and Institutional Plant Programme;
- National Programme on Improved Chulhas;
- Integrated Rural Energy Programme;
- Wind Energy Programme;
- Biomass Power Programme;
- Biomass Resource Assessment Programme;
- Biomass Gasifier Programme;
- Small Hydro Programme; and
- Energy Recovery Programme.

The Ministry of Non-conventional Energy sources has so far invested Rs.18,000 crores for promotion and development of renewable energy sector in the country. The financial allocation for the development of the sector has increased from 0.1 per cent of the total outlay during the sixth plan to 0.44 per cent in the Ninth Plan. The total installed capacity from renewable, which stood at meagre 36MW at the end of the Seventh Plan, has now risen to 3409MW. In order to undertake various programmes indicated above, during 10th plan, an total outlay of Rs.10289.33 crores is proposed.

Conclusion

Renewable energy sources such as solar, wind, biogas, biomass, ocean thermal, tidal, wave, small and micro-hydel are perennial, unlimited, and environmentally friendly in nature. These forms of energy can adopt decentralized and favourable energy option for sustainable village development. Panchayat Raj Institutions can opt for these energy sources in decentralized manner. The villages are dependent only on agricultural production could now divert their attention towards establishment of rural industries that can considerably make use of renewable energy technologies. Establishment and promotion of rural industries could along save the villages. Agriculture and rural industries could complement to each other. The renewable energy technologies could pave the way easily for such integration.

Making villages more livable is a favourite concept of Mahatma Gandhi. His dream of gram swaraj and swadeshi can be achieved through utilization of locally available resources and thus village can attain self sufficiency. Gandhi recommended decentralization of power through a combination of State ownership in a few fields and village ownership and trusteeship in the rest of the economy. He said "The heavy machinery for work of public utility... would be owned by the state... The village communities would own powerhouses". The time is not too far way to realize the dreams of Mahatma Gandhi which will come true in the near future, for which, the Ministry of Non-conventional Energy Sources has been working towards to achieve the dreams of our Father of Nation.

REFERENCES

Common, M. : *Environmental and Resource Economics* (Longman, Harlow, 1996). Kirk, G (ed) : *Schumacher on Energy* (Abacus, London, 1983).

Lockeretz, W. : *Agriculture and Energy* (Academic Press, London, 1977).

Mahajan, V.S. : *Studies in Energy and Economic Development* (Deep and Deep, New Delhi, 1991).

Pradeep Chaturvedi : *Bio-Energy Resources — Planning, Production and Utilisation* (Concept, New Delhi, 1995).

Reliance : *Reliance Review of Energy Market* (Reliance, Mumbai, 2003).

World Bank : *World Development Report 2001-02* (World Bank, Washington D.C., 2002)

11

Human Resource Management in Small Scale Industries

H. SANKARAN

An organization with human resources only can exist or co-exist. These are some of the questions whose answers lie in the subject of Human Resource Management (HRM). But before we attempt to understand how an organization should manage its human resources, we need to answer the generic question, what is management and then we can understand what is Human Resource Management?

What is Management?

Management is the process of efficiently getting activities completed with and through other people. The management process includes the planning, organizing, leading, and controlling activities that take place to accomplish objectives. Human Resource Management is concerned with the 'people' dimension in management. Since every organization is made up of people, acquiring their services, developing their skills, motivating them to high levels of performance, and ensuring that they continue to maintain their commitment to the organizations are essential to achieving organizational objectives. This is true, regardless of the type of organization-government, business, education, health, recreation, or social action. Getting and keeping good people is critical to the success of every organization, whether profit or nonprofit, public or private.

Personnel to HRM

Personnel departments were once called 'Health and Happiness' departments. The people assigned to deal with personnel issues were often individuals who where past their prime. The personnel department was seen as a place where less-productive employees could be placed with minimal damage to the organization's ongoing operations. Individuals in the personnel department were perceived as those responsible for planning company picnics, vacation schedules, and retirement parties. Personnel, as an activity, were seen as a necessary, but unimportant, part of the organization. Yet as the field of management began to mature, more emphasis was being placed on the workers. Various studies revealed that recognizing workers for the work they had done could influence their productivity. Workers were becoming more demanding in what they wanted from a job; and society, by means of laws and legislation, was placing new demands on employers. No longer could the personnel department be treated as a detour on the road to success. Organizations had to hire the best-qualified candidate without regard to race, religion, colour, and sex.

HRM Model

In recent years there has been relative agreement among HRM specialists as to what constitutes the field of HRM. The model, that provided the focus, was developed by the American Society for Training and Development (ASTD). In its study, ASTD identified nine human resource areas :

(1) Training and Development
(2) Organization and Development
(3) Organization/Job Design
(4) Human Resource Planning
(5) Selection and Staffing
(6) Personnel Research and Information Systems
(7) Compensation/Benefits
(8) Employee Assistance
(9) Union/Labour Relations

These nine areas have been termed spokes of the wheel in that each area impacts on the human resource outputs: quality of work life, productivity, and readiness for change. Fig.11.1 is a representation of this model, and the focus of each spoke. The outputs of this model–quality of work life, productivity, and readiness for change-warrant further exploration.

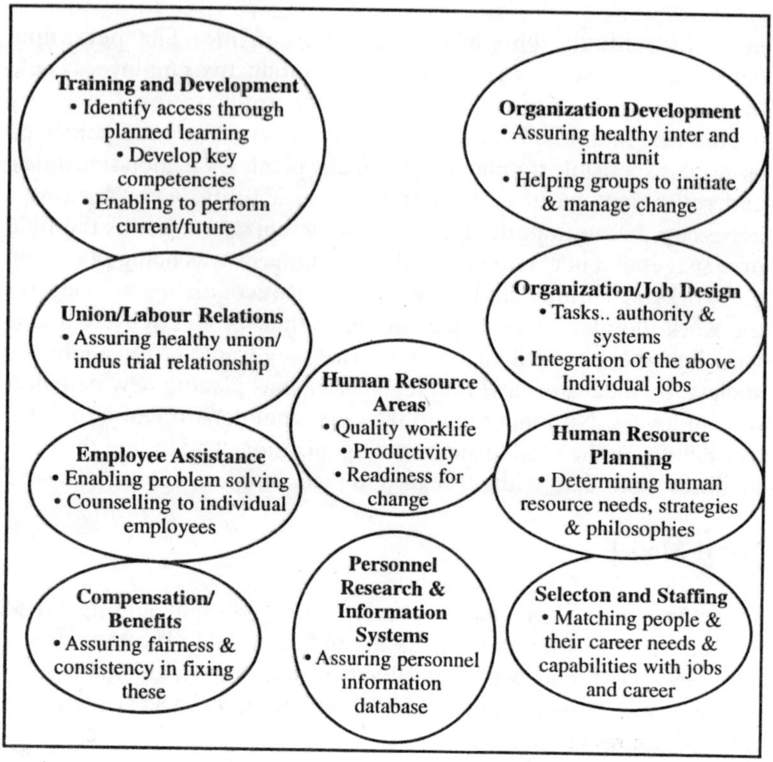

Fig. 11.1 : Human Resource Wheel

Definitions

In order to define the terms "Tiny Industry/Enterprises", "Small Scale Industries" and "Medium Size Industries", we refer to the various decisions and interpretations given by the Appropriate Government taking into account various aspects like Investment on plant & machinery, employees employed and other related matters pertaining to fiscal support/credit support along with infrastructure support.

Definition of SSI

After analyzing the concept of SSI in detail, basic question may arise, as to why an official definition is required at all? The policy of the Government is to encourage SSI for various socio-economic reasons.

In support of the Government offers several facilities-promotional, developmental and financial. To ensure that only the genuine SSI units are benefited, an official definition has become a necessity for implementing the programmes.

Definition-1955 – Small Scale Industries Board

"A unit employing less than 50 persons, if using power and less than 100 persons without use of power, and with capital assets not exceeding Rs.5 lakhs".

Definition-1960 – Small Scale Industries Board

"Small Scale Industries will include all industrial units with a capital investment of not more than Rs.5 lakhs irrespective of the number of persons employed".

Definition-1966 – Ministry of Industry, Government of India

"Small Scale Industries will include all industrial units with a capital investment of not more than Rs.7.5 lakhs irrespective of the number of persons employed. Capital invested for this purpose will mean investment in plant and machinery only".

Definition-1974 – Small Scale Industries Board

"Undertakings have investments in fixed assets in plant and machinery not exceeding Rs.10 lakhs.

Definition-1980 – Industrial Policy Resolution– Government of India

"The limit of investment in small scale units was raised from Rs.10 lakhs to Rs.20 lakhs.

Definition-1985 – Industrial Policy Resolution– Government of India

"Small Scale Industries will include all industrial units with a capital investment of not more than Rs.35 lakhs; irrespective of the number of persons employed".

Definition-1991- Industrial Policy Resolution – Government of India

"An industrial undertaking in which the investment in fixed assets in plant and machinery, whether held on ownership terms or no lease, or by hire purchase, does not exceed Rs.60 lakhs.

There are four main classifications of Small Scale Industries in India, namely (i) manufacturing, (ii) feeder, (iii) servicing and (iv) ancillary industries.

Concept of Small Scale Industry

The concept of SSI in the Indian context is vague for two reasons. Firstly, it is hard to draw a distinction between a traditional cottage industry and a small scale industry of today; and secondly the definition of SSI given by the Government has been undergoing frequent revisions. The origin of the concept of SSI in India can be traced as far back as to that of the Industrial Commission of 1968 which defined the SSI as an "organised industry carried on in workshops or factories having simple operations with a provisional character". As a matter of fact, this is just similar to the present modern concept of SSI which draws a distinction between the factory and the non-factory sector. Shah stated that no satisfactory definition of a SSI could be attempted by any authority in the country. He suggested that SSI or cottage industry may be understood as an enterprise engaged in a series of operations carried on by workmen skilled in their craft and on their own responsibility, the finished product of which he markets himself. The worker works in his own home, use his own tools and materials and provides his own labour or at the most the labour of such members of his family as are able to assist him.

This concept is mostly akin to that of the modern village and cottage industries though not similar to the SSI of today. In the views of Jawaharlal Nehru, "Small Scale Industry units may be those which have (a) no mechanical power but hired labour of below 10 persons; or (b) mechanical power with less than 10 h.p. and with or without hired labour.

According to the Working Group on Industry and Economic Commission for Asia and Far East (ECAFE), a small scale unit is one which operates mainly with hired labour usually not exceeding fifty workers and not using any motor power in any operation or with hired labour of 20 workers or so and using power. Here the main emphasis is on the number of workers and on the use of motor power, but output is not at all considered. Further the Committee on Finance for Private Sector defined the SSI units as those units which are not identified with the agricultural economy and in which the investment of capital and labour are relatively small. i.e., units with assets, say between Rs.0.10 and Rs.5.00 lakhs engaged largely in the production of articles that are ancillary to or competitive with the products of the so-called large scale industries. This definition clearly indicates that the SSI units are different from cottage industries.

At one time, the Government grouped small industrial undertakings into two categories – those using power but employing less than 50 persons and those not using power but employing less than 100 persons. All small enterprises had a capital investment of less than Rs.5 lakhs. The criterion of the number of persons employed, however, was considered as descriptive, as the figures of fifty and hundred persons were purely arbitrary.

Human Resource Management in Small Scale Industry

To tool at HRM more specifically, we suggest that it is a process consisting of four functions-acquisition, development, motivation, and maintenance – of human resources. In less academic terms, we might describe these four functions as getting people, preparing them, activating them, and keeping them.

Acquisition Function

The acquisition begins with planning. Relative to human resource requirements, we need to know where we are going and how we are going to get there. This includes the estimating of demands and supplied of labour. Acquisition also includes the recruitment, selection, and socialization of employees.

Development Function

The development function can be viewed along three Dimensions. The first is employee training, which emphasizes skill development and the changing of attitudes among workers. The second is management development, which concerns itself primarily with knowledge acquisition and the enhancement of an executive's conceptual abilities. The third is career development, which is the continual effort to match long-term individual and organizational needs.

Motivation Function

The motivation function begins with the recognition that individuals are unique and that motivation techniques must reflect the needs of each individual. Within the motivation function, alienation, job satisfaction, performance appraisal, behavioural and structural techniques for stimulating worker performance, the importance of linking rewards to performance, compensation and benefits administration, and how to handle problem employees are reviewed.

Maintenance Function

The final function is maintenance. In contrast to the motivation function, which attempts to stimulate performance, the maintenance function is concerned with providing those working conditions that employees believe are necessary in order to maintain their commitment to the organization.

Within the confines of the four functions—acquisition, development, motivation, and maintenance—many changes have occurred over the years. What once was merely an activity to find a warm body to fill a vacancy has become a sophisticated process of finding, developing, and retaining the best-qualified person for the job. But this metamorphosis did not occur overnight. It is the result of many changes in management thought, society and the workers themselves. Let us now look at this transition of personnel.

Organization of HR Department in Small Scale Industry

Two issues become relevant in a discussion on organization of an HR department. They are (i) place of the HR department in the overall set-up and (ii) composition of the HR department itself. The Table 11.1 explains HRM objectives and functions.

Status of the HR department in the total organizational structure depends on whether a unit is small or medium. In most of the small organizations, there is no separate department to coordinate the

Table 11.1 : HRM Objectives and Functions

HRM objectives	*Supporting functions*
1. Societal Objectives	1. Legal compliance
	2. Benefits
	3. Union management relations
2. Organizational objectives	1. Human resource planning
	2. Employee relation
	3. Selection
	4. Training and development
	5. Appraisal
	6. Placement
	7. Assessment
3. Functional objectives	1. Appraisal
	2. Placement
	3. Assessment
4. Personal objectives	1. Training and development
	2. Appraisal
	3. Placement
	4. Compensation
	5. Assessment

activities relating to personnel. In fact there may not be any personnel managers at all. Services of outsiders who specialize in maintaining accounts and records relating to provident fund pension and other statutory requirements are retained for a fee. Alternatively, a low-placed employee may be entrusted with the task of attending to these functions. The figure following this para shows a structure of this type. In fact it was this arrangement, which was followed in the past, irrespective of the six of the organization. Earlier, personnel departments were called health and happiness departments. The people assigned to deal with personnel issues were often individuals who were past their prime. The personnel department was seen as a place where the lesser productive employees could be placed with minimal damage to the organization's ongoing operations. Individuals in the personnel department were perceived as those responsible for planning company picnics, vacation schedules and retirement parties. Personnel, as an activity, was seen as a necessary but unimportant part of the organization. Fortunately, things have changed for the better, and the status of the personnel department has improved enormously over the years.

HRM in a Small-Scale Unit

In a small scale unit, HRM plays a role through the proprietor/owner as well the executives handling different types of process-wise activities. The Personnel Department is ordinarily manned by the Office Manager designate himself. Taking into account the overhead cost (fixed overhead), the Small Scale Industries do not consider keen attention to allot a person or more than a person exclusively for the purpose of transforming HR policies and functions thereupon. Moreover, Small Scale Units have been emerged from the Tiny Scale level and hence, the same conventional approach applicable will be adopted when the Units reach the level of Small Scale Unit.

The following chart shows the HRM profile of the Small Scale Units :

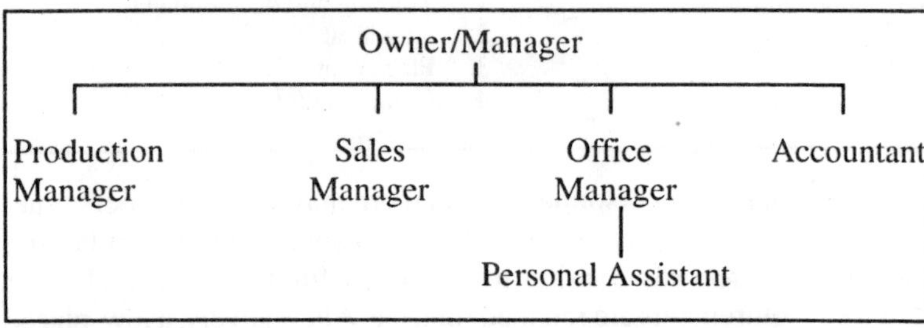

Fig. 11.2 : Organisational Structure

Composition of a HR/Personnel Department

The HR/Personnel Department ordinarily consists of a separate ancillary organisation structure comprises of a Director-Personnel/ HRM or General Manager-Personnel/HRM, as the case may be (depends upon the respective norms of the organisation concerned) to Head the Human Resources Development Department. Further the said Head delegates the functions and responsibilities pertaining to Personnel, Administration, Labour Welfare, Public Relations, Industrial Relations and HRD divisions/departments. Normally, Personnel Department deals with Salary Administration, Maintenance of Records pertaining to Statutory matters as well the Social Security Measures warranted basically. I.R. Department deals with matters relating to disciplining the employee, counselling, negotiating with the work force on matters relating to salary fixation, working conditions, fixation of work norms and other monetary benefits. H.R. Department deals with manpower planning, placement, training, performance appraisal, rewards & recognition. Labour Welfare/ Administration Departments handle the affairs relating to welfare, canteen, housekeeping, other basic facilities like drinking water, toilet, etc. The following chart shows the composition of HR/Personnel Department in the Industrial Units, for the sake of achieving results in transforming the human potentials available in to expected results/ output targeted by the concerned employer/proprietor, as the case may be.

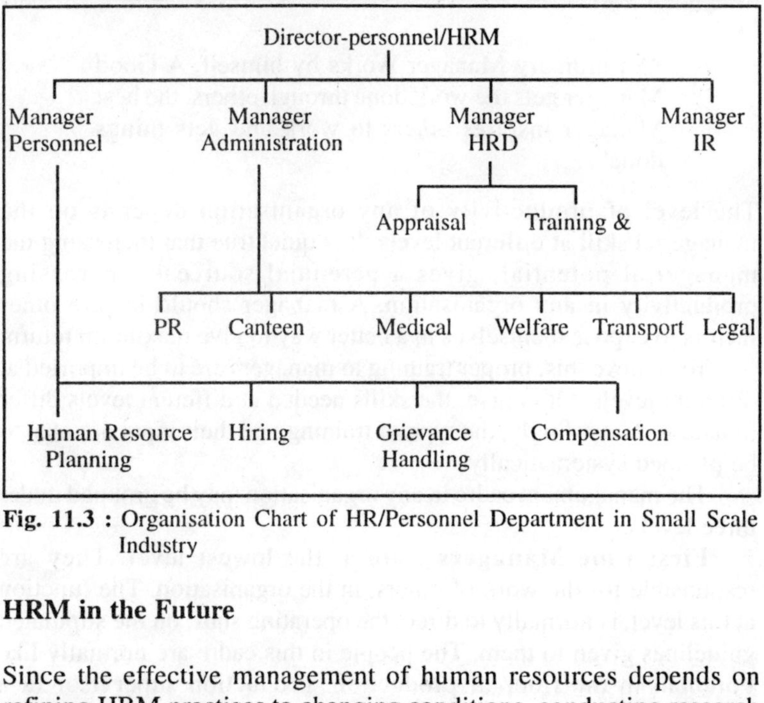

Fig. 11.3 : Organisation Chart of HR/Personnel Department in Small Scale Industry

HRM in the Future

Since the effective management of human resources depends on refining HRM practices to changing conditions, conducting research and keeping an eye on the future. Research allows the manager to keep abreast of the latest findings in HRM and provides a framework by which solutions to unique HRM problems can be found. We look at past trends and attempts to extend them to the end of this century. This is done in the belief that HRM is a dynamic and changing field. The successful manager will be at the forefront of these changes with new and relevant HRM practices.

12

Managing the Managers

K. AIYADURAI

> "An ordinary Manager Works by himself, A Good Manager gets the work done through others, the best Manager inspires others to work and gets things done".

The level of productivity of any organisation depends on the managerial skill at different levels. It is quiet true that increasing the managerial potential, gives a perennial source of increasing productivity in any organisation. A manager should inspire other factors to expose themselves in a better way to give maximum return.

To achieve this, proper training to managers are to be imported at different levels. Of course, the skills needed at different levels differ in nature. Accordingly, the type of training and their input are also to be planned systematically.

The management cadre in any organisation may be grouped under three levels.

First Line Managers : are at the lowest level. They are responsible for the work of others, in the organisation. The function at this level, is normally to direct the operating staff, on the stipulated guidelines given to them. The people in this cadre are normally like Foreman in the floor of production. Production supervisor in a manufacturing plant, Technical Supervisors at the department levels, office Superintendent, and so on. The job at this level is, allocation of work to subordinates and to work with them, to supervise them.

Middle Level Management : is the second cadre in the management. Here, the managers are to implement the organisational policies towards achievement of the organisation goals. In this process, the activities of first line managers are to be directed and supervised closely. Functional managers like Finance Manager, Production

Manager, etc., function under this category. The responsibility at this level is to balance the demands of the superiors with the capacities of the subordinates.

Top Level Management : is the function of setting organisational goals and establishing operating policies. This level also guides the organisation's interactions with its environment. The overall responsibility of 'Managing the Managers' also is an important function at this level.

Generally, Managers come to such position normally by means of :

(a) Hereditary Succession
(b) Promotion from subordinate level
(c) Qualified occupation by merit or proving their success
(d) Accident.

Whatever may be the means through which they occupy, they must have some basic professional training on some vital skills.

These skills can be grouped under three basic heads *viz.* Technical Skill, Human Skill, Conceptual Skill.

Technical Skill refers to knowledge and aptitude towards the use and adoption of technology and tools in the specialised field.

Human Skills is the ability to work with, understand and motivate other people, either as individuals or as groups. Human relations and behavioural aspects are the major components in this skill.

Conceptual Skill is the mental ability to take decisions and implement them, by co-ordinating and integrating all the interest and activities of the organisation. A manager needs enough conceptual skills, to recognise how the various factors in a given situation, are inter related, so that the action he takes will be, to the best interest of the entire organisation.

All the three skills are essentially required to the managers, at all the levels. But the manager must be able to co-ordinate their relative importance on the basis of his level in management.

Relative Skills needed for effective performance at different levels of management can be well understood by observing the following diagram.

First Line Management	*Middle Management*	*Top Management*
Conceptual Skill Human Skill Technical Skill	Conceptual Human Skill Technical	Conceptual Human Technical

These skills may be acquired by proper training and experience.

Training Inputs at Different Levels of Management Cadre

First Line Managers

The major input for the people at the lower level management cadre are identification of organisational goal and target and the methodology to advise them, Interpersonal relationship, Group Psychology, Industrial and Labour Laws Knowledge on the performance of other similar units, and so on.

These are to be inducted by on the job training, through their immediate supervisors and through other experts who are familiar in psychology and on legal matters. People at this level will be normally coming to this position with experience as subordinates in the same organisation or in other units. Their past experience and the present induction will make them more efficient in their way of work.

Middle Management Cadre

People at the middle management level are to be trained periodically on organisational methods, inter-personal relationship, general psychology, leadership qualities, knowledge on comparative performance of similar units, technological development in their respective functional areas, and so on.

The methodology of training the managers at this level may be through conducting workshops or seminars with experts, facilitating interaction with people in the similar cadre in other organisations, encouraging participation in professional bodies and associations, provision of multimedia contact, organising interdisciplinary exchange programmes for self learning and so on.

Top Level Management

Training input at this level may be on decision making skill, organisational skills, professional management, Information Technology, Recent development in respective field, knowledge on various functional areas in Management, exposure to marketing orientation and quality consciousness and so on.

The methodology for training top level managerial personnel may be through arrangement of :

- Creating self interest in learning things.
- Association with equal cadre in other units.
- Association with subordinates.
- Familiarising past records.
- High level short term training at Management training institutions.
- Exposure to multimedia for information.
- Through workshops/seminars by participation with experts in other areas.
- Leadership training and social activities.
- Awareness about government policies and changes at the global level.
- Participation in industry – institution programmes.

These steps would give positive response in increasing the efficiency of the people at the higher level. When the managers are equipped with such skills, it will be automatically passed on to the subordinate level. This will keep the organisation ever vibrant.

13

Entrepreneurship Attitudes of PMRY Beneficiaries

V. GOPALSAMY

Entrepreneur

Richard Cantillon was the first to introduce the term 'entrepreneur' and defined as the agent who buys means of production at certain prices in order to combine them into a product that he is going to sell at prices that are uncertain at the moment at which he commits to his costs.

According to Evans entrepreneurs are persons who initiate, organise, manage and control the affairs of a business unit that combines the factors of production to supply goods & services whether the business pertains to agriculture, industry trade, or profession[1].

Attitude

Attitudes are feelings and beliefs that eagerly determine how one will perceive his environment, commit himself to intended actions and ultimately behave. Attitudes are mental sets that affects how a person will view something else, much as a window provides a framework for purview into or out of building.

In short attitudes are evaluative statements or judgements concerning objects, people or events[2].

Objective

In India unemployment exists in both rural and urban areas and among both uneducated and educated[3].

There is an absolute increase in unemployment among the educated which took place in the category of Matriculates, Higher Secondary, Graduates and Post Graduates but the percentage of unemployed matriculates has always been the highest.

To reduce unemployment, the Government of India has introduced and implemented various schemes such as Employment Guarantee Scheme, National Rural Employment Programme, Rural Landless Employment Guarantee Programme, Integrated Rural Development Programme, Jawahar Rozgar Yojana, Self Employment among Unemployed Youths etc[5].

Now in the recent budget (1999-2000), the self employment programmes for the rural poor to be merged into one and called Swarna Jyanthi Gram Seva - Rozgar Yojana. The PMRY Scheme was not disturbed by the Finance Minister since it is a mile stone among employment generation programmes. PMRY is a laudable attempt of the Government of India to tackle the twin problems of the unemployment among educated youth and lack of entrepreneurship in the country[5].

On realising these facts the author has made some attempts to study the attitude of the PMRY beneficiaries towards the scheme. The author has considered the two definitions as guidance and conducted a survey among the PMRY beneficiaries (entrepreneurs) about their attitudes towards the PMRY scheme in and around Dindigul Town with an objective to bring out facts relating to the motivating factors of the budding entrepreneurs, credit assistance required to them, the relative role played by the various institutions, the importance of the training programme and the various hurdles in the way of success in the PMRY scheme. The study will help the related institutions in the assessment of the effectiveness and the efficiency of PMRY in developing the young entrepreneurs in the field of Small Scale Industries.

Out of 630 beneficiaries of PMRY scheme in Dindigul town it has been decided to select a sample of size 93 (15 per cent of the size of the population) using the random sampling method. An elaborate questionnaire has been administered to the beneficiaries by the researcher.

Findings of the Study

(i) The age of the beneficiaries varied between 18 and 35 years the mean age being 28.

(ii) The mean annual income of the beneficiaries is observed to be Rs.14,806.45.

(iii) About 82 per cent of the beneficiaries have felt that the training is necessary and important to them.

(iv) Previous experience has been the major motivating factor in starting small business unit.

(v) Majority of the respondents have come to know of the scheme and the availability of loans through DIC and banks.

(vi) About 92 per cent of the beneficiaries have obtained loans from banks and the rest from other financial institutions such as TIIC, NABARD and NSIC.

(vii) In the assessment of the project cost, officers of banks, DIC and CED have helped them.

(viii) The mean value of the initial costs of the project all the beneficiaries has been estimated as Rs.56,881.72.

(ix) The mean value of the initial costs of the project recommended by the task force committee is found to be Rs.55,161.29.

(x) The mean value of the initial costs of the projects sanctioned as loans by the banks is calculated as Rs.50,332.58.

(xi) On an average, DIC took about 37 days for the approval of the projects.

(xii) On an average, the beneficiaries had to visit the loan sanctioning banks for about 7 times.

(xiii) About 75 per cent of the respondents had to wait in the bank from 30 to 45 minutes to meet the bank officers. In their view, 4 to 5p.m. is the ideal time to meet the bank officers in connection with their loan applications.

(xiv) Most of the beneficiaries have felt the need for training after sanctioning of loans.

(xv) About 36 per cent wanted the training programme to concentrate on marketing, 27 per cent on psychological contents, 14 per cent on managerial aspects and the remaining on legal aspects.

(xvi) Most of the beneficiaries want to have field visits and market surveys in the training programme.

(xvii) About 53 per cent of the beneficiaries were of the view that the loan is sanctioned only to persons already in business.

(xviii) About 36 per cent of the beneficiaries could get loans on the basis of security deposit, 27 per cent without any security 18 per cent on immovable property, 11 per cent on recommendations and 8 per cent on personal security.

(xix) 90 per cent of the beneficiaries took less than 40 days to prepare the documents needed by the bank.

(xx) Beneficiaries had to spend more time to get no objection certificate for the bank and legal opinions.

(xxi) The average expenditure incurred in the process of getting loans has been Rs.480.

(xxii) Availability of marketing facility and labour had been the major factors determining the location of the business unit.

(xxiii) The small scale business started by them has been profitable to 72 per cent of the beneficiaries. About 63 per cent of the beneficiaries were repaying the loans regularly.

(xxiv) About 82 per cent of the beneficiaries have felt the need for follow up assistance after sanction of loans and provision of training.

(xxv) About 94 per cent of the beneficiaries were satisfied with the assistance rendered by DIC. About 87 per cent were satisfied with banks and 96 per cent with Centre for Entrepreneur Development a nodal agency of Government of Tamil Nadu, Madurai.

(xxvi) About 55 per cent of the beneficiaries had the view that the existing age limit may be continued. About 66 per cent of the beneficiaries were satisfied with the prescribed minimum educational qualification.

(xxvii) Economic condition of the business units and repayment of loans are associated.

(xxviii) There is an association between previous experience of the beneficiary and the successful running of the business unit.

Suggestions

The above salient findings of the study enable the researcher to make the following suggestions to improve the scheme :

(a) The existing loan limit of Rs.1 lakh may be enhanced.

(b) The time taken by DIC in processing and approving the applications may be reduced.
(c) Effort may be taken to reduce the time taken by the banks in issuing no objection certificate.
(d) The course contents of the training programme may be strengthened with more emphasis to marketing, field visits and market surveys.
(e) Follow-up assistance may be strengthened further.
(f) The scheme may be extended by increasing the number of beneficiaries.

Suggestion for Further Study

A research study may be conducted on the pattern of investment, income and employment generated, capital output ratio and profit earned by the beneficiaries a PMRY in Dindigul District.

REFERENCES

1. Ruddar Datt and Sundaram, K.P.M., *Indian Economy*, S.Chand and Company Ltd., New Delhi, Eighth Edition, 1998.
2. Gupta, C.B. and Srinivasan, N.P., *Entrepreneurial Development,* Sultan Chand & Sons., New Delhi, Third Edition, 1995.
3. Fred Luthans, *Organisational Behaviour,* McGraw Hill.
4. Government of India, *Entrepreneurship in Small Scale Industries,* Ministry of Industry, New Delhi, 1977.
5. *The Hindu*, Volume No.122, No.9, Dated the 28th February 1999.

14

Withdrawal of Women from Entrepreneurship

Causes and Remedies

S. GANESAN

The traditional perception of women as a helper in the occupation of the husband and a homemaker is gradually vanishing in the recent past. Women have started proving themselves in many fields including entrepreneurship and their participation in entrepreneurial activities has increased by leap and bound. Quite a large number of women entrepreneurs have set up their enterprises and have been in business successfully. Though majority of women entrepreneurs work at either micro level or tiny/cottage sectors, presence of women as owners in large scale enterprises are not uncommon.

The realisation that women are a valuable human resources has been gaining ground and their crucial role in human development through child rearing and support services at home, recognition of women's services as a necessary sub-system of the entire socio-economic system are gradually becoming a part of modern attitudes.

Women have been successful in breaking their confinement within the limits of their homes by entering into varied kinds of professions and services. Women entrepreneurs have proved to be on par with their men counterparts in business acumen and are emerging as smart and dynamic entrepreneurs.

Many factors and developments have influenced women to take up entrepreneurship. The success of White Revolution has identified the closeness of women to animal husbandry. In most of the States, particularly in Gujarat, women own a majority of milch animals. The advent of labour saving technology is another very important socio-economic development. Such technology frees women from the drudgery of long labour. The acceptance of the small family concept and the resultant break-up of traditional joint family system have resulted in psychological liberation experienced by women. The successive industrial policies of the government have laid greater emphasis on the development of women entrepreneurship in the country. A large number of entrepreneurship development programmes especially for women have been conducted over the years, thus motivating women to become entrepreneurs. A related development is the introduction of special cells and schemes by financial institutions for catering to the financial needs of prospective women entrepreneurs. Improved level of women education has increased the aspirations to widen their horizon and extend their role. More women, now, opt for higher technical and professional education as the educational facilities increase in the country. Proportion of women in the labour force has also increased as result of this. All these factors and developments have influenced women to take up non-traditional higher levels of activities (like that of entrepreneurship) apart from their conventional role of homemaking.

The Alagappa Institute of Management has taken up a major research project to identify the motivational factors and to assess the success rate of women entrepreneurs in Tamil Nadu. As a part of the project, the Institute organised a Focus Group Meeting of women entrepreneurs with the objective of getting to know about their experiences as entrepreneurs. The meeting, which was attended by 16 women who tried entrepreneurship, provided a lot of information on the motivational factors, style of functioning, and problems faced by them. This paper discusses the causes for the withdrawal of women from entrepreneurship apart from touching upon the problems faced by them, heavily drawing information provided at the Focus Group Meeting.

Problems Faced by Women Entrepreneurs

The problems faced by women entrepreneurs in the country emanate from a multitude of sources and are manifold. These problems can be classified under three broad categories *viz*., personal, social, and economic.

Personal Problems

The lack of experience, lack of adequate technical knowledge, lack of business exposure, and conservative attitude towards risk taking are some of the personal problems of women entrepreneurs. Women have been traditionally doing the service jobs in business enterprises. Back home, they have been involved only in activities concerning home-making. A majority of the households do not consult women in major decisions resulting in a situation where women lacked experience in managing major problems individually. Another related problem is the lack of adequate technical knowledge on the part of women. Humanities and arts programmes have traditionally been in great demand by women students. Women students were not encouraged to take up technical programmes as the society was of the opinion that the women were not suitable to such programmes. There has been dearth of women technicians in the country, though the trend is changing for good recently. As already stated, women were not involved in taking major decisions – be they relate to family or family business. This again has resulted in the lack of business exposure to women. Women, in general, seem to have a conservative attitude towards family and business. It is hard to convince an average women to accept to changes. This quality of risk and change aversion worked against women in their development.

Added to all these, are the physiological problems women face. The fragile structure of the body, menstruation, pregnancy, need to tender infants, and the likes are some of the problems specific to women. Working women have the option of taking leave—subject to limitations – when they face such 'problems'. Women entrepreneurs do not afford to go on leave during the crucial phases of the ventures.

Social Problems

Women in general face a lot of problem in the male-dominated society. There are many unwritten rules, which the society scrupulously follows. Nobody in the society dare to violate any of these unwritten rules for fear of social boycott. Most of these rules pertain to women and encompass a wide variety of social activities like women's interaction with others, women's education, their employment, hours of work, dress, outings, and the like. Women can interact only with known persons. The socicty talks ill of a woman who moves freely with 'outsiders'.

Hours of Work

Women are considered as the weaker sex and subtle. There is also a belief that women can not withstand longer hours of work, and works at odd hours. The legal environment of the country prohibits organisations from employing women after the evening and before dawn. This environment is not congenial to women to take up those entrepreneurial ventures, which demand lot of their time at odd hours. Women here can become successful entrepreneurs only when either they have an enabling workforce behind them or the venture itself can be taken care of at their own time.

Economic Problems

Till recently the women in India did not have legal rights in their parental properties. The women had to satisfy with the 'Stridhan' provided to them at the time of their marriage. The relevant Act has now been amended to recognise the rights of women in the parental properties. However the change in the legal framework in favour of women sharing family properties with their brothers has not been recognised in the major part of the country. Women did not have properties in their names (with the exception of few cases), since only men members of the families have owned family properties. Women could not provide any collateral security for their loans in the absence any properties. This presented women in poor light in the eyes of the banking system. The banks insist the husband or father sign the documents, when a woman applies for loan. Women in India and many of the developing countries face innumerable problems, as they do not possess any economic power.

Causes for Withdrawal

It has been observed that a majority of women who enter into entrepreneurship with lot of enthusiasm close their business units within about three years of operation of the business. A variety of reasons are behind this behaviour and a number of factors play behind the scene. The causes for withdrawal of women from entrepreneurship and the factors which force them to do so, identified at the Focus Group Meeting are explained below :

Social Factors

Women as entrepreneurs have to successfully cross a lot of impediments put by none other than the society to which they belong. As discussed in the earlier pages, the social outcasts just because they have to have interaction with others. The situation is not uncommon even in metropolitan cities of the country. Women may have to move with many persons in multitude of groups like customers, suppliers, creditors, etc., as an entrepreneur for getting things done for the business. Women find it difficult to have even business relationship with 'others', due to the hostile social environment. There may not be any difficulty for women entrepreneurs who operate on a large scale in an organised sector because they can afford to employ professional executives for taking care of the business operations. Moreover the society accepts the violation of social norms by women in the higher echelons of the society. Similarly the women entrepreneurs operating at micro level – like street vendors, petty shop owners, etc. – do have very less problems with the society, as the society does not care about them. It is only the women at the middle level who face a lot of problems in their professions or enterprises. Society seems to be very harsh to the women at the middle level.

Most women do not have their own choice even in the matter of education. A large proportion of rural girls drop out from schooling in their early ages. The choice of educational programmes of the middle class women is restricted to arts and humanities subjects. Even those who venture out to professional programmes in engineering and technology have difficulty in getting suitable employment commensurate with their education. Instances of technically qualified women taking up employment at clerical level are very common.

Employment

While men do not have much problem in taking up employment of their choice, women in India and other Asian countries face lot of problems in getting suitable employment. The organisations prefer women to be employed at staff level. Very less number of women is employed at the executive level. The number of women who are employed at production facilities as technicians are very few and far between. Moreover women can not have free mobility to take up employment at far away places. All this have resulted in a societal belief that women are suitable only for providing service to the men-dominated societal systems. When a woman dares to enter into a technology driven entrepreneurial venture, she faces many impediments even in the normal course of management of the enterprise.

Society looks a woman entrepreneur suspiciously as she moves with the outside world without any inhibitions for the purpose of the business. The has set a value for women: what is expected of them and what not is expected. There are lot of social curbs on women to have relationship with other men outside the family. This poses a serious problem for women entrepreneurs, as they have to move freely with the outside world for business development and survival. Movement of women without a family companion is also not encouraged by the society. Stories will be built about the modesty of a woman who travels frequently without a family companion.

There is all the likelihood that a woman who start her enterprise before her marriage will close down the business on her own after the marriage due to many reasons. The husband may not like his wife to have a business of her own. Even if the husband is willing, his parents– who may live in a distant place – may be totally against it. The woman may have to close down the business, as she has to move with her husband to a distant place. She may have to close down the business when she is pregnant and/or to look after the children. This type of closure is sure to occur especially when the family members are indifferent to her business.

Personal Factors

A majority of the women entrepreneurs withdraw from business due to shear lock of experience. The problem of lock of experience is also compounded by the problems of lack of adequate technical skill, lack of exposure to business risks, and lack of managerial capabilities. These problems, which have been already discussed in the earlier pages, act as the factors contributing to the decision for withdrawal from business.

Women are also unable to attend to the needs of her business at all times due to her engagement as family-maker. Many a time, women entrepreneurs fail to attend to the problems of their businesses as and when they arise. The problems connected with this factor has already been discussed.

Neighbourhood women entrepreneurs tend to close their business just because they lose interest in business. This may be due to many reasons like huge bad debts, inability to compete with the regular entrepreneurs, neighbourhood politics, etc.

Neighbourhood women entrepreneurs start their business in-house with abounded enthusiasm that is short-lived. They get unlimited encouragement from the family members, neighbours, and friends initially. They also get business assistance like purchase, selling, spread of information about the business, and to a certain extent collection. But all these are only for the initial period. After a while, may be after 2 or 3 years, the interest in the business is lost for everybody including the entrepreneur.

Economic Factors

Women fail in business also due to the lock of economic empowerment. Women are not given a share in the family properties, in spite of the existence of legal framework favourable to women in this regard.

Women are not able to offer any collateral security when they apply for loans from the organised sector for the simple reason that no family property is in her name. Even if she has a property in her name, she may fail to get the permission from either in-laws or husband for offering the property as collateral security. This necessitates borrowing from unorganised sector at a hefty rate of interest making the return from business unattractive.

Remedy

Development of entrepreneurship by women in our country heavily depends on removing all the above personal, social, and economic problems. Most of these problems could not be solved within a short period, since they involve changing the societal values and tradition with respect of women. The government can take up some of the economic problems immediately for their redress. The society and the government have to undertake many concerted efforts before an enabling environment is created for developing women entrepreneurs in large number.

Women entrepreneurs have a lot of problems in managing their businesses. Women have to face innumerable problems even for entering into entrepreneurship. The problems faced by women to start their businesses can be classified into three categories, *viz.*, personal problems, social problems, and economic problems. All these problems as told by women entrepreneurs in a Focus Group Meeting organised by the author as part of a major research project on motivational factors of women entrepreneurs are discussed in this paper.

It has been observed that most of the women entrepreneurs tend to close their businesses within very short period of time due to varied reasons. The reasons include lack of experience, indifference on the part of the family members including husband, moving to a distant place due to marriage, lack of expertise in financial management, inability to attend to the problems of the business as when they arise, and inability to 'move out' either for canvassing orders or for business follow-up. The list of the causes for the withdrawal of women from entrepreneurship is endless. The society need to look at the problems of women entrepreneurs and do something to rectify the environmental conditions so as to ensure faster growth of women entrepreneurs.

15

Emergence of Women Managers in the HRD Scene

An Analysis of the Myths and Realities About Women Managers

P. Vaijayanthi and K. Meena

This paper focuses on the reasons for paucity in growth of women managers and their career problems. It includes a statistical presentation of women managers all over the world, a review of the impediments to their growth - the various organizational and social practices and attitudes and a primary data study of women managers in Tiruchirapalli, Tamil Nadu. Suggestions and implications have been drawn from the findings of the study.

"Woman is the companion of man, gifted with equal mental capacities, she has the right to participate in the minutest details of the activities of man, she has the same right to freedom or liberty as he..... By sheer force of a vicious custom, even the most ignorant and the worthless men have been enjoying a superiority over women which they do not deserve & ought not to have" - Gandhiji "*Young India*" (1918).

I. Problem Setting

Although women constitute over fifty per cent of the world's population, in no country do they represent half or even close to half of the corporate managers.

In Japan, women play a much larger managerial role in small and medium enterprises, more than 25000 women are company presidents, whereas large corporations have less than 1 per cent of women managers.

In 1986, only 1.6 per cent of the companies had women above the rank of division managers, 4 per cent had women upto the level of division managers, 21.6 per cent had women upto section heads and 22.8 per cent upto sub section heads.

Out of 420 companies surveyed in the Western European countries, 50 per cent had not employed any women managers, 8 per cent of managers were women in U.K., 9 per cent in France and 13 per cent in Portugal. There were no women in the top management of the companies in Netherlands, Germany and Italy.

The British Institute of Management reports that women in the same positions as men on an average are paid less by 3000 pounds a year at the middle management level. Women managers in Singapore receive lower salaries than men. In Israel, the policies are midway between European and Middle Eastern countries. The main thrust is the women's role, as the mother and the housewife.

Baroness Lackwood, the immediate past chairwoman of the equal opportunities Commission of U.K. says that, "Women at the top are still noticeable by their scarcity. Only 9 per cent of Managers are women".

In Canada and U.S. 25 per cent of all Managers and 9 per cent of the senior Managers have been found to be women.

In Soviet Russia, companies prefer married men in top positions. All over Europe, many of the top female executives are with the U.S. Companies. Seeing the successful performance of American women managers in Banks, Britain has been increasingly hiring women for the banks.

In India, till two decades ago, women did not join the corporate world. Till 1948, there was prohibition against women taking higher civil service examination and even when it was ended only unmarried women or widows without encumbrances could join the services. According to the 1991 census, the proportion of women is 6 per cent in all civil services, 7.5 per cent in I.A.S. and 10 per cent in the Foreign Services. Women had entered the corporate sector only in the late sixties and had worked only in the area of Public Relations and Labour Welfare. There were very few in the main line functions of marketing and finance. In the seventies, areas of market research and Human resources development saw the entry of women. Banks have been recruiting them but women managers constitute only upto 6 to 7 per cent in sharp contrast to being 30 to 35 per cent of the workforce. The early eighties witnessed an increasing number of women chartered accountants and their induction, for the first time into the area of industrial relations. Some women joined research and development cells also.

The trend in the nineties, is that women are making their marks in production area and General Management. Women managers seem to be more comfortable in Hi-Tech business environments, in the electronics and computer software industries. The growth rate of women in the banking and finance profession, as a whole has been faster than that of men, as confirmed by the discussions and deliberations of the National Conference organised by the All India Management Association. Between 1960 & 1980 recruitment of women has risen from 25 per cent to 68 per cent .

According to the Human Development Report 1996, only 2.3 per cent of Administrators and Managers are women in India, against the world average of 14 per cent . In U.S.A, their percentage is 42. The above statistics is an indication of the wide gap that exists between the professed philosophy of equality and the present reality. It also indicates the long and rough journey that women may have to traverse to achieve equality of status and opportunity in the real sense.

The reasons for the paucity of women in Management are fairly similar world wide. Cultural sanctions, educational barriers, legal restrictions, corporate obstacles and women's disinterest in pursuing managerial careers have been listed as dominant constraints.

In the sixth plan (1980 - 1985) there was a shift from welfare to development approaches for women. This plan recognized women's lack of access to resources as an important constraint to her development. Women's Welfare and Development Bureau was set-up under the Ministry of Social Welfare in 1976, to initiate women development.

The National Commission for women was constituted vide the National Commission for Women Act, 1990 and assigned with responsibilities; one of which was to review the safeguards provided to women under the constitution and other laws and make recommendations for amendments, to remove all inadequacies and short comings in these safeguards.

II. Objectives of the Study

(1) To identify and verify the causes for the paucity in the growth and the low proportions of women in managerial positions.

(2) To learn the problems and impediments in the career growth of women manager.
(3) To identify and to confirm the managerial aptitudes and capacities in women occupying managerial positions.
(4) To identify if any, the links between the family background and the career of women.

III. Reasons Identified for Paucity in Growth of Women Managers and their Career Problems

The various reasons that have impeded the entry of women in the managerial arena can be classified into three.

- Inhibitions and set backs in women
- Social and Cultural attitudes and practices
- Prejudices practices and attitudes of the Professional world

A. Inhibitions and Set Backs in Women

Lack of proper education and protected nurturing of women from their childhood along with restrictions in behaviour and liberty right from childhood had provided limited exposures of reality to women. Hence women generally have been found to have the following self inhibitions which impede their growth in career :

- Feel they are secondary at the work place, family and society
- Risk averse - due to lack of informal power
- Shun achievement for fear of being taken away from the family
- Doing the job well but caring less for success
- Less career oriented to accommodate husband and family
- Low commitment
- Fall apart in crisis
- Rules minded
- Control Oriented
- Feeling of guilt (for not caring for the family)

B. Social, Cultural Attitudes and Practices

The following social and cultural myths and attitudes about women have impeded the growth of women in their career :

- Women are created to be soft and nurturing
- Women's work is in the house
- Those who work outside neglect children
- Limited social life
- Cannot entertain friends
- Male chauvinism which expects her to take up jobs for economic reasons, but does not appreciate her accepting top status in the organization and society.
- Discouragement of single-women.
- Restrictions to literacy.
- Sheltered grooming of girls.
- Conservatives restrict women from public-related assignments.
- Blocked mobility.

C. Practice, Prejudices & Attitudes of the Professional World

The following attitudes about women in organizations impede their career growth :

- Married women and mothers are not reliable workers
- Women are afraid of achievement
- Poor at qualitative analysis
- Unable to make tough decisions
- Training for women is wasteful.
- Discrimination in promotional practices
- Discrimination in training facilities
- Limited overall growth opportunities
- Sex role stereotyping-categorising certain jobs for women.

Apart from the above discussed attitudes and myths that work against her, woman has certain problems due to her triple role of mother, wife and professional. Being a woman manager sometimes create problems very specific to women. Following are some of the *problems in career*.

- Additional pressure at work due to —
  (a) *Tokenism* - only a few women make it to the senior positions, because of which she is noticed by all.
  (b) Compelled to outwit others.

- Lack of experience in the politics of the job.
- Experience *role conflict* - when balancing between career and personal lives.
- Pressure of *role-switching* – When she switches from autonomy and authority in her career to secondary roles at her home
- Male domination
- Resentment of male colleagues and subordinates
- Inability to travel
- Success not attributed to merit
- Cannot attend duty in odd hours
- Male members take undue advantage of women
- Broken services due to child bearing
- Promotion opportunities affected by parenting.

IV. A personal Study of Women Managers their capabilities and Problems in Tiruchirapalli, Tamil Nadu

Methods

A sample of 50 women managers and fifteen managers of women managers. [(ie) *Superiors of women Managers*] were contacted and opinions elicited to infer on problems faced by women managers and learn about the professional attributes claimed to be exhibited by women managers. Information was obtained through structured questionnaires and interview schedules. Opinions and views about social attitudes and impediments to the growth of women managers were also elicited from opinion leaders like retired management professionals, educationists, active members of women organizations and members of the "Forum of women in public Sector".

Sample Design

Proportion of the sample

Women managers from banking sector	10
From Public Sector Organisations	30
From Private Organizations	6
Entrepreneurial woman managers	4
Total	50

Personal opinions were elicited form 50 women managers from the following public sector organisations, private firms and entrepreneurial managers, in and around Tiruchirapalli town.

1. Bharat Heavy Electricals Ltd.
2. Tamilnadu Telecommunications Circle - Trichy Telecom District
3. The State Bank of India.
4. The Indian Overseas Bank
5. The Indian Bank
6. The City Union Bank
7. Women Entrepreneurial Managers

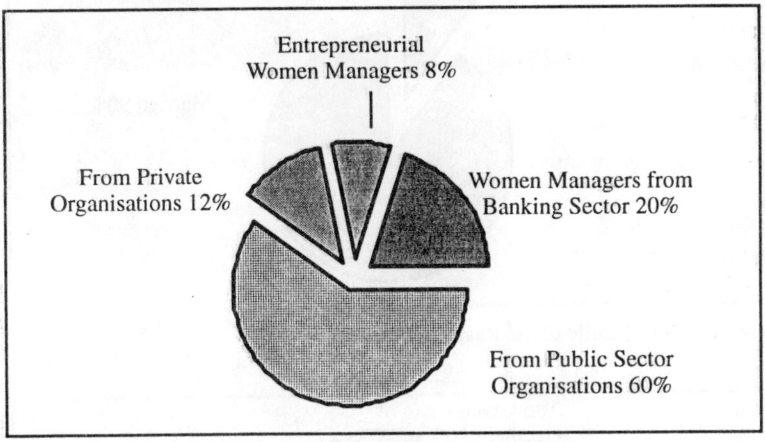

Graph 15.1 : Composition of the Sample Women Managers

Fifteen Managers of Women Managers were also contacted from the various organisations listed above to obtain their views about their subordinate women managers.

Some Statistics on Women Managers in Triuchirapalli, Tamil Nadu

The State Bank of India at Trichy (including its branches at Trichy and Karur districts) has one woman manager and two women officers out of a total of 192 officers. The Indian Bank, including its branches at Trichy, Periakulam & Karur district has no women managers. It has 7 officers in the whole of Trichy. The Indian Overseas Bank also has *no women* managers in Trichy area. There are two women officers out of 350 officers at this bank. The City Union Bank also has no women managers in its branches at Trichy. There are four women junior managers and 20 women officers in this bank.

The Tamil Nadu Telecommunications Circle, Trichy Telecom district, has two women managers, one at the top management level and the other at the Junior Management sevel.

The Bharat Heavy Electricais Ltd., Trichy Unit, has 48 women managers out of a total of 1700 junior, middle and senior level managers.

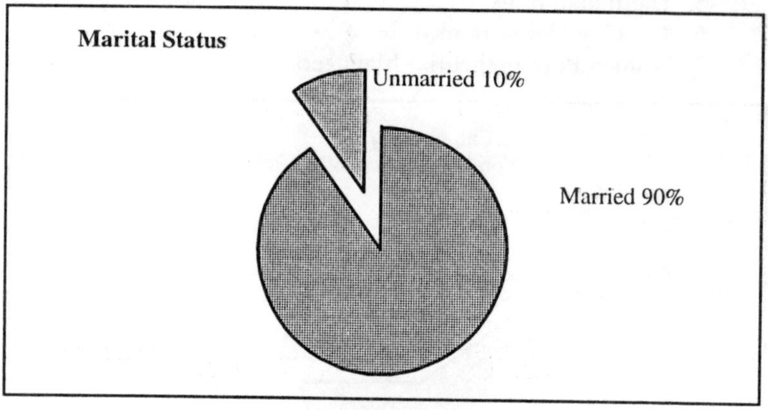

Graph 15.2 : Profile of the Respondent Managers

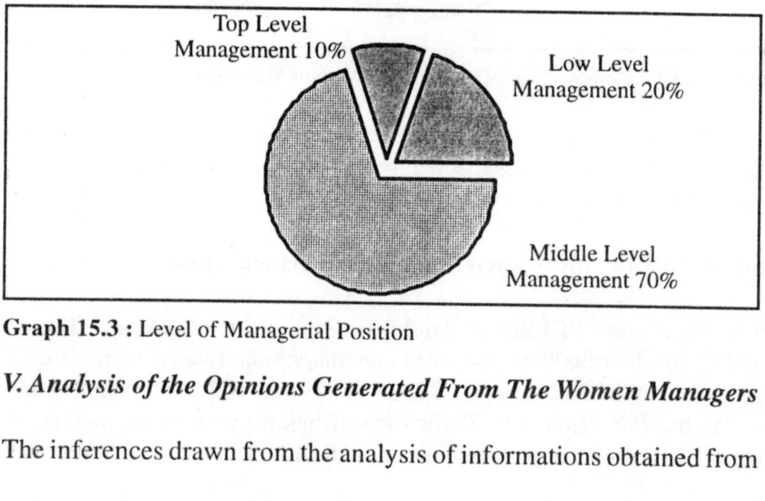

Graph 15.3 : Level of Managerial Position

V. Analysis of the Opinions Generated From The Women Managers

The inferences drawn from the analysis of informations obtained from the respondent women managers, superiors of women managers and opinion leaders have been presented below as findings.

VI. Findings Relating to the Managerial Capabilities of Women Managers

The following are the positive and negative attributes of women managers as opined by their superiors :

- Women have high self-esteem and higher drive for achievements (90 per cent of the superiors)
- Men and Women Managers are equally good in decision making (100 per cent)
- Men and women are equally good in learning, empathising and problem solving (90 per cent)
- Women do not have tenacity to withstand work stress (20 per cent)
- Women lack emotional stability (100 per cent)
- Women cannot be delegated with tasks related to the shop-floor mass (100 per cent)
- Gender discrimination does not influence promotion decisions (90 per cent)
- There is no specific relationship between the family background and the career of women.

VII. Findings Relating to the Career Problems of Women Managers

The inferences drawn form the opinions of women managers about their career problems are presented below :

- Women are individualistic and do not accept the traditional sex stereotype jobs (100 per cent).
- Majority of the women are supported *by* men in the household chores.
- Women sacrifice career goals for family commitments like parenting (100 per cent).
- Subordinates resent being led by women managers (40 per cent).
- Superiors provide support to women and are either paternalistic or participative (90 per cent).

- Have felt isolated and watched at because of male domination (30 per cent).
- Women are not prepared to give up their Jobs on account of their family(100 per cent).
- Experience difficulties due to dual role of family and career (100 per cent).

Views of the Opinion Leaders

The opinion leaders have felt that women are far assertive and individualistic in their career decisions. They no longer accept sex-bias to affect their career. Most of the assertive and talented women professional come back to gain a big time in the career after a break to accommodate parenting (about five years). Gender discrimination does not affect the career life of women at managerial levels.

The proportion of women managers in high managerial positions are very low due to the social and cultural norms of the society a few decades back. Women should learn to be more updated in informations and try to spend more time for self-development. They should learn to be more committed and should not be tempted to sacrifice career ambitions for the standard feminine rewards like marriage.

VIII. Suggestions

To Parents :

- Parental upbringing should bring out leadership traits in girls.
- Avoid discriminated behaviour reinforcement by parents.
- Women themselves must be committed to their advancement.

To Organisations :

- Machinery for sharing information like networking
- Advancement of women should be made as a institutional commitment.
- Corporate settings-to encourage women's mobility to the top.
- Inner mentor-inner circle support to facilitate to learn the rules of the game
- Women-friendly policies.
- Flexitime

- Part-time work schedules
- Alternate day jobs
- Work from home
- Flexible work options
- Opportunities for developing interpersonal skills.
- Hiring by clusters to prevent tokenism.

IX. Future Implications

The findings of the study show a very positive sea-change in the acceptance of women in the managerial echelons :

- In ten to fifteen years women might be at par or excel men in managerial positions.
- Women are more committed to career and are increasingly entering the managerial arena.
- Social changes are in support of career women.
- Younger people are becoming more liberated husbands sharing responsibilities of child care and home-making.
- Gender discrimination in the work environment is falling to influence.
- Organisations have responded by developing women-supporting policies.

X. Conclusion

In some countries over the last two decades, the percentages of women in management have increased, but in none have they approached equality.

Organisations do not exist in vacuum. They are mere extensions of the society. Vast changes in the cultural and social norms will surely have their impact on the attitude towards women in management. Demythologising the society is possible only when all the pillars - the parents, the policy makers, the governing boards and MEN resolve to change.

16

The Labour Cost as an Input Related to Output in Khadi and Village Industries

S. RADHAKRISHNAN AND K. BALASUBRAMANI

It is now an established fact that the Khadi and Village Industries sector has an important role to play in the economy of the country. This sector today claims to have created jobs for more than 6 million people in the rural areas, and its contribution in rural industrialisation is of great significance.

In the early stages of the planning process, the Khadi and Village Industries commission was assigned a Crucial role for the upliftment of the rural poor. Unfortunately due to scarcity of funds and other constraints, the sector has not received the primacy and priority it deserved, whereas the large scale industries have shown as faster growth than the KVI sector.

The economic reforms initiated by the Government of India have produced a new dynamism in the economy through liberalisation and globalisation but inspite of all this we must protect small and tiny sector from Multi National Corporations (MNCs), so that unequal are not treated equally in the process of economic development. Too much emphasis on "open economy" may not create conditions for favourable economic growth of the nation. The country is not yet ready to face the implications of free competition for parties of unequal economic strength. Therefore, in the initial stages of "open economy" the protection of Khadi and village industries is needed. The Central Government must function as the national organisation for taking care of national interests in all matters, so that justice, social, economic and political as envisaged in Indian Constitution can become a reality to all Indian citizens.

In order to bring out the importance of labour in the production of Khadi and Village Industries Sector, a study is undertaken.

The share of cost of labour in the value of KVI production is said to be 50 per cent . From this study it is once again proved beyond doubt that major value of production goes to labour and there by centralisation of wealth and power is minimised as envisaged by Mahatma Gandhi.

Labour as a Factor of Production

Labour is the most important ingredient in the process of product. In other words, labour is one of the most important factors of production.[1] It is labour which involves multitude of human beings whose active collaboration is definitely needed for the smooth production and development of an industry.[2] So labour as a factor of production is an inevitable input in every business and industrial sector. It is more true in the case of Khadi and Village Industries.

The relationship between cost of labour - input and value of production (VP) - output both at the price level of 1986-87 is studied in this chapter. The percentage of cost of labour on V.P. and the mean average of all the above three items are also examined. The analysis carried out for all the five institution under study for a period of 12 years from 1986-87 to 1997-98 and tabulated in Tables 16.1 to 16.5.

Employment Problems of Developing Country

Today, many developing countries are plagued by historically unique combination of massive rural - to - urban population movements, stagnating agricultural productivity, and growing urban and rural unemployment and under employment. The incidence of unemployment is much higher among the young and increasingly among more educated in the 15-24 age bracket. Even larger fractions of both urban rural labour forces suffer from under employment. They have neither the complementary resources (if they are working full time) nor the opportunities (if they work only part time) for increasing their very low income to levels comparable with those in modern manufacturing, commerce and the service sector. Because of its relationship to the problem of third world poverty, the employment issue occupies a central place in the study of under development.

The employment problem in third world countries therefore has a number of facts that make it historically unique and thus subject to a variety of unconventional economic analysis. There are three major reasons for this :

(i) Unemployment and under employment regularly and chronically affect much larger proportions of LDC. Labour forces than unemployment did in the industrialized countries, even during the worst year of the great depression.

(ii) The world employment problems have much more complex causes than employment problems in developed countries. They therefore require a variety of policy approaches that go far beyond simple keynesian - type policies to expand aggregate demand.

(iii) Whatever the dimensions and causes of umemployment in third world nations, it is associated with human circumstances of object poverty and low levels of living such as have rarely be experienced in the now developed countries. There is no urgent need for concerted policy action by both the less developed and more developed nations. As we shall see, the LDCs need to readjust domestic policies to include employment creation as a major social and economic objective, while the developed countries need to review and readjust their traditional economic policies vis-a-vis the third world, especially in the area of trade, aid and technology.[3]

Unemployment Problem in India

India is saddled with the problems of unemployment and under-employment. But under employment is more pronounced in rural areas. Generally employment for the jobless, vocations for the under employed, prospective pursuits to those who have completed their professional courses, generation of work to fight poverty are the topics that have been discussed, debated, analysed and elucidated. Often many occupations which keep the persons busy for eight hours, according to many, cannot be accepted as employment and self employment.

As far as, the rural areas are concerned, land less labour, share - croppers, traditional artisans, small and marginal farmers constitute the indigent section.

Actually what we see is not total unemployment but more under - employment. Any village for that matter will have only a very small percentage of total unemployment. Mostly this would be the product of a faulty system of education. Some may have completed a course and entered the employment market. Their education has absolutely nothing to do with the kind of jobs they are seeking. To an extent they remain unemployed. Since they are very selective and will not have any job often enough they are more unemployable rather than unemployed.[4]

Unemployment in India

Unemployment is almost a universal feature of capitalistic societies. In India, there has always been a serious degree of unemployment as well as under employment and it constitutes one of the most serious problems. It is merely the massive dimensions of the problem that is frightening, but the most alarming feature of the unemployment situation is that it is deteriorating from year to year. Unemployment problem, today, is increasing at the rate of one lakh more jobless persons every month more rapidly than ever in the past.[5] The total number of unemployed on the live registers of the employment exchanges went up still further to 580 lakhs as on 1995. It is expected to increase to 940 lakhs in 2002. A.D.[6]

KVI and Cost of Labour

There is no denying the fact the Khadi and Village Industries have enormous job potentiality with low rate of investment. But they suffer from numerous bottlenecks. State support in the reservation and purchase preference for Khadi and Village Industry products are all the more necessary, apart from the exemption of labourer laws etc. Given a boost, KVI programme will generate employment to the people in the far-flung villages which will invariably augment their income and income would create demand and this would lead to substained growth. This will reflect to real development of rural areas, a dream the Government endeavours to realise.[7]

Under these circumstances, for our rural areas Khadi and Village Industry, cottage industry, handicrafts, tiny and modern small scale sectors can be the major source of employment. Technological innovations can widen employment base in the KVI sector as they will attract new entrants.[8] Because Khadi designs are outdated and techniques are old. In other cases, the cost of production becomes high and the rural industrial products cannot compete with the products produced in the large scale sector.[9] The Khadi and Village Industries face a number of problems which are massive both quantitatively and qualitatively. There are problems such as the balance of payment, the issue of money inflation, poverty and unemployment inequalities in income and distribution and asset ownership and etc.[10] Normally the calculation of labour cost is in consistent with the minimum wage act. Every employer must, therefore, be asked to pay the full cost of labour which at its minimum should be such that the worker and his family can purchase at prevailing market prices all those goods and services without which they cannot live with human dignity. The supreme court approved the six following guidelines for fixing the minimum wage :

(a) the standard of working - class family
(b) minimum food requirement
(c) clothing requirements should be estimated at a per capita consumption
(d) in respect of housing
(e) fuel, lighting and other miscellaneous items of expenditure should constitute
(f) children's education, minimum recreation old age, marriage etc.

So, the supreme court finally observed, " the wage structure which approximately answers the above six components is nothing more than a minimum wage at subsistence level. The employees are entitled to the minimum wage at all times and under all circumstances. An employer who cannot pay the minimum wage has no right to engage labour and no justification to run the industry.[11]

The foregoing point out the wage and benefits are the rewards and price of labour. The labour cost is the cost of all manpower employed in the factory. Labour cost naturally is a function of the number of employees and the rate of remuneration.[12]

Labour Productivity in KVI

Generally labour productivity techniques are not strictly followed in KVI sector. Because they do not have an idea of how to apply technical measurement tools and benefits of labour productivity. The application of labour productivity tools in the Khadi and Village Industries would definitely bring some benefits. These benefits are listed below :

(1) Reduction in the prices of services and goods produced; higher possibility of exports and foreign exchange earnings.
(2) Higher turnover of goods at low prices would trigger demand in the market.
(3) Higher profits for the organisation (industry).
(4) Increase in earnings of the employees and higher employment opportunities.
(5) Improved economic conditions and enhancement of national wealth as well as per capita income.
(6) Rise in the standard of living and quality of living.

Normally productivity is the key to prosperity and workers have a great role to play in increasing and promoting productivity.[13]

Calculation of Labour Cost

The requirement of labour and thereby the number of workers depends on the number of operators/helpers required for operating the various machines and manning of various services. The number of supervisory personnel and administrative staff may be calculated on the basis of the general norms prevailing in the industry. In estimating remuneration rates, the prevailing rates in the industry / area should be taken into account. The remuneration should include, besides basic pay, dearness, medical reimbursement, bonus payments etc. In addition it should also take into account the vacations, overtime work, night work, work on holidays etc.[14]

Statement of the Problem

Conversion of raw material into finished goods needs so many inputs such as labour, machinery, technical know - how etc. In large scale industry the labour factor will be meagre when compared to the tiny sector. The production process in the large scale sector is designed in such a way that it reduces the labour factor and in the place of labour sophisticated machines and tools are installed. The cost of machines at the initial stage may be high. But in the long run it will be reduced to Zero. The investment made on machinery will be recovered with in a stipulated time and afterwords the cost of machine will be zero and profit will be abnormal. If machines are replaced with labour, the cost of labour will be increasing every year and the productivity may be the same and thus the question of earning abnormal profit as stated above is not possible. Industries with profit motive are trying to reduce the labour factor and install machinery, so that more profit is earned in the long run.

In the tiny sector, especially in Khadi and Village Industries the major objective is to provide employment by employing more number of people in the place of machinery. However, they are allowed to use simple machines and tools in order to reduce the drudgery and increase the efficiency of the labour. In large scale industries, the cost of both direct and indirect labour may range between 10 and 15 per cent. In the case of khadi and village industries the cost of labour may range between 30 and 45 per cent which includes production wages to spinners, weavers, artisans salary to the supervisor, manager and other office staffs, EPF contribution and other perks and fringe benefits given to them.

Statistical Tools

Inter temporal comparison of performance needs estimate of variations in variables over a period of time. For this purpose, a number of statistical tools are available. They are :

(a) Mean average,
(b) Simple averages of annual growth rates,
(c) Co-efficient of correlation,
(d) Regression and
(e) Linear programming.

Correlation analysis is used to understand relationship between labour cost and value of production. Regression and regression line analysis discussed closely related on labour cost and value or production, we can find out the expected value for a certain amount of labour cost and value of production.

Data Available on the Issues

The study covers a period of twelve year from 1986-87 to 1997-98. During the period general price level has gone up bringing down real value of money. Data on value of production, cost of labour for the period under review are available in current prices. These data do not

Table 16.1 : Labour Cost and Output, Gandhigram Khadi and Village Industries Public Charitable Trust - Gandhigram. (Whole sale Price Index - Base year 1986-87 - 138 points)

(Rs. in lakhs)

Year	*Labour Cost*	*Percentage of growth rate*	*Whole sale Price Index*	*Labour cost at The price level of 1986-87*	*Percentage of growth rate*	*Value of production*	*Percentage of growth rate*	*Production value at the price level of 1986-87*	*Percentage of growth rate*	*Share Percent-age 5/9*
1	2	3	4	5	6	7	8	9	10	11
1986-87	52.50	–	138.0	52.50	–	150.08	–	150.08	–	34.98
1987-88	57.10	8.76	148.5	53.06	1.07	193.09	28.66	179.44	19.56	29.57
1988-89	60.43	5.83	154.2	54.08	3.28	193.70	0.32	173.35	(-) 3.39	31.20
1989-90	71.71	18.67	165.7	59.72	10.43	236.95	22.33	197.34	13.84	30.26
1990-91	80.13	11.74	182.7	60.53	1.36	302.00	27.45	228.11	15.59	26.54
1991-92	87.71	9.46	207.8	58.25	(-)3.77	258.22	(-)14.50	171.48	(-)24.83	33.97
1992-93	84.63	(-)3.51	228.7	51.29	(-)11.95	288.34	11.66	173.99	1.46	29.48
1993-94	78.82	(-)6.87	247.8	43.89	(-)14.43	269.86	(-)6.41	150.29	(-)13.62	29.20
1994-95	78.99	(-)0.22	274.7	39.68	(-) 9.59	281.65	4.37	141.49	(-)5.86	28.04
1995-96	110.00	39.26	295.8	51.32	29.33	337.97	19.20	157.67	11.44	32.55
1996-97	122.74	11.58	314.6	53.84	4.91	424.05	25.46	186.01	17.97	28.95
1997-98	116.92	(-)4.74	329.8	48.92	(-)9.14	354.20	(-)16.47	146.21	(-)20.40	33.46
Total	1001.68	90.40		627.08	1.5	3290.09	102.07	2055.46	11.76	368.20
Mean	83.47	8.22		52.26	0.14	274.17	9.28	171.29	1.07	30.68
Co. efficient correlation = 0.5630Y = a+bx				a = 52.56 bx = 1.43				a = 171.29 bx = 4.97		

Source: The Statement of Final Accounts of the above Institution.

lend themselves for inter temporal comparison, since one rupee of 1986-87 is not equal to one rupee of 1997-98. Therefore, the data in current prices have been converted to constant price level (1986-87). For this purpose Whole Sale Price Index of all commodities with base year of 1986-87 has been used as deflator.

In Adequacy of Data

The concept of ex-factory value of production has certain limitations. It includes of labour, and inputs secured by the institutions understudy from others. Since the institutions understudy made no contribution to the cost of labour input their inclusion in the ex-factory value of output will exaggerate the contribution of the institution towards value creation.

Data Analysis

The production value of KVI goods consists of two major components one is cost of raw material and the other component is labour. The capital invested in the KVI is meagre. The interest on capital invested in Khadi and Village Industries is normal at 4 per cent and for khadi interest free loan is provided. The two components as stated above that is the raw material and labour together accounts for 80 to 85 per cent. In the preceding chapter the share of RM input on VP is studied now in the present chapter cost of labour or labour input and the value of production will be analysed.

Inference

GKVIPCT

The particulars of labour cost and growth etc., are furnished in the table 16.1. The cost of labour in current prices during the period of twelve years has almost doubled in current prices and there is know change noticed in the constant price (deflated value). It clearly denotes that the real value of wages has not increased in the past twelve years. But in terms of money value there is 100 per cent growth rate. It is understood that there is no change in the standard of living of workers over a period of twelve years, as there is no increase in the real value of wages.

Cost of Labour

The cost of labour increased in the year 1989 - 90 for about 11 lakhs, it consists of 5 lakhs of production wages and other fringe benefits. The beneficiaries of enhanced wage bill are the direct labourers like spinners, weavers of this institution. This is also linked with productivity and there is an increase of Rs.43.25 lakhs of production. It is once again proved that increased wage benefits to the labour who are directly involved in production will certainly increase the productivity. The same trend is noticed in the year 1990-91 also. When we look at the overall picture, the cost of labour increased at the rate of Rs.1.43 lakhs every year during the period under review.

Value of Production *Vs* Labour Cost

The value of production in current prices is found to be increasing and in constant price it is stabilised with ofcourse some variations in the mid period. The correlation analysis reveals that there is a positive relationship between the cost of labour in deflated value and the value of production. However the correlation is very moderate as the r-value is only 0.5630.

Share of Percentage

The percentage of labour cost in the total production value ranges between 27 and 35. The mean average cost of labour is Rs.30.68 Lakhs.

Mention here may be made that in the KVI sector the wages may be normally more than 40 per cent . In GKVIPCT, besides khadi more number of VI activities have been undertaken. Especially in P.C.P.I. oil industries labour cost will be only 6 to 10 per cent and the major share goes to raw materials. The khadi production is around 30 per cent on the total production of the above institution. Hence, the percentage of labour cost on total value of production accounts for 30.68 per cent.

MNSS

The particulars relating to cost of labour, value of production, etc are furnished in Table 16.2.

Table 16.2 : Labour Cost and Output, Madurai North Sarvodaya Sangh - Palani. (Whole Sale Price Index - Base year 1986-87 - 138 points)

(Rs. in lakhs)

Year	*Labour Cost*	*Percentage of growth rate*	*Whole sale Price Index*	*Labour cost at the price level of 1986-87*	*Percentage of growth rate*	*Value of production*	*Percentage of growth rate*	*Production value at the price level of 1986-87*	*Percentage of growth rate*	*Share Percent-age 5/9*
1	2	3	4	5	6	7	8	9	10	11
1986-87	16.01	-	138.0	16.01	-	31.25	-	31.25	-	51.23
1987-88	15.65	(-)2.25	148.5	14.54	(-)9.18	36.99	18.37	34.38	10.02	42.29
1988-89	13.78	(-)11.95	154.2	12.33	(-)15.20	33.04	(-)10.68	29.57	(-)13.99	41.70
1989-90	21.63	56.97	165.7	18.01	46.07	43.06	30.33	35.86	21.27	50.22
1990-91	28.54	31.55	182.7	21.56	19.71	57.14	32.70	43.16	20.36	49.95
1991-92	31.43	10.13	207.8	20.87	(-)3.20	68.43	19.76	45.44	5.28	45.93
1992-93	31.58	0.48	228.7	19.06	(-) 8.67	70.09	2.43	42.29	(-)6.93	45.07
1993-94	33.67	6.62	247.8	18.75	(-)1.63	78.51	12.01	43.72	3.38	42.89
1994-95	32.01	(-)4.93	274.7	16.08	(-)14.24	77.89	(-)0.79	39.13	(-)10.50	41.09
1995-96	49.07	53.30	295.8	22.89	42.35	129.09	65.73	60.22	53.90	38.01
1996-97	57.66	17.51	314.6	25.29	10.48	119.49	(-)7.44	52.41	(-)12.97	48.25
1997-98	65.67	13.89	329.8	27.48	8.66	138.61	16.00	58.00	10.67	47.38
Total	396.70	171.32		232.87	75.15	883.59	178.42	515.68	80.49	544.01
Mean	33.06	15.57		19.41	6.83	73.63	16.22	42.97	7.32	45.33

Co. efficient correlation = 0.7931 Y = a+bx

a = 19.41, bx = 0.61 (column 5)

a = 42.97, bx = 4.11 (column 9)

Source : The Statement of Final Accounts of the above Institution.

Cost of Labour

There was no significant increase in the cost of labour at current price level upto 1994 - 95. There was a sudden increase in the cost of labour and as well as production from the year 1995-96 to 1997-98 under the study. The regression analysis using the least square technique revealed that the cost of labour appreciated year often years by Rs.0.61 lakhs.

Cost of Labour on Value of Production

The same trend is noticed at deflated price. The mean average cost of labour at deflated price was 19.41 and the value of production was 42.97. It is estimated that cost of labour is 45 per cent of the total value of production in deflated price. In the case of current price level also it has recorded 44.9 per cent in the total production. The r-value being 0.7931, we can say that the relationship between these two variables is highly positive and the cost of labour has great influence on the value of production.

Share of Percentage

The percentage of cost of labour on value of production has been calculated for every year under study and the mean average was found to be 45.33. Hence, it may be concluded that the labour input on total value of production is 45 per cent in MNSS.

The growth rate of labour cost and value of production are also calculated in both current and deflated prices. There is no remarkable increase in the growth of cost of labour in both the prices upto 1994 - 95. In the year 1994-95 onwards there is significant increase in the cost of labour due to increase in the production wages. It is also noticed that there is corresponding increase in the VP. This is said to be the healthy trend as there is increase in the production for every wage increase and hence this wage increase is productivity linked.

It is further pointed out that the higher increase of production wages in the year 1995 - 96 (Rs.14.40 lakhs) has brought a corresponding increase in VP (Rs.51.20 lakhs). This is due to production of value added products like silk sarees.

GSS

The particulars of cost of labour and value of production in GSS are furnished in table 16.3.

Cost of Labour and VP

The cost of labour and value of production for a period of twelve years understudy are almost stagnant except in the year 1994-95. There is no significant increase in both the factors. Rather a negative growth rate is noticed in more than five years both in cost of labour and VP. With regard to the relationship between cost of labour and VP it is estimated that the mean average of labour cost at deflated prices is Rs.3.31 lakhs and the VP is Rs.14.73 lakhs. The value of production is 4.5 times of the cost of labour. It is so because, the main line of production of this institution is VI products. Through the labour cost fluctuated during the years understudy, it recorded an annual growth rate of Rs.0.15 lakhs per annum. A highly positive relationship exists between these two variables in the organisation (r-0.8775).

Share of Percentage

As stated earlier the cost of labour in VP will be less than 10 per cent and in case of khadi it is more than 40 per cent. In other four institutions understudy the cost of labour ranges from 35 per cent to 45 per cent where the major activity is khadi production.

In GSS main line of production is non-edible oil, soap and oil industries. They have started undertaking Khadi activities at meagre level from the year 1986-87 onwards.

KSS

The particular relating to the labour cost and VP etc., of Karur Sarvodaya Sangh are furnished in the table 16.4.

Cost of Labour

Perusal of this table reveals that the cost of labour has undergone a major change in the year 1995-96 as there is productivity linked wage

Table 16.3 : Labour Cost and Outpur Gandhi Seva Sangh - Chattrapatti. (Wholesale Price Index - Base year 1986-87 - 138 points)

(Rs. in lakhs)

Year	*Labour Cost*	*Percentage of growth rate*	*Whole sale Price Index*	*Labour cost at the price level of 1986-87*	*Percentage of growth rate*	*Value of production*	*Percentage of growth rate*	*Production value at the price level of 1986-87*	*Percentage of growth rate*	*Share Percent-age 5/9*
1	2	3	4	5	6	7	8	9	10	11
1986-87	1.76	-	138.0	1.76	-	18.36	-	18.36	-	9.59
1987-88	2.14	21.59	148.5	1.99	13.07	16.87	(-)8.12	15.68	(-)14.60	12.69
1988-89	4.82	125.23	154.2	4.31	116.58	20.07	18.97	17.96	14.54	24.00
1989-90	5.43	12.66	165.7	4.52	4.87	23.34	16.29	19.44	8.24	23.25
1990-91	7.32	34.81	182.7	5.53	22.35	25.81	10.58	19.49	0.26	28.37
1991-92	4.69	(-)35.93	207.8	3.11	(-)43.76	23.29	(-)9.76	15.47	(-)20.63	20.10
1992-93	3.48	(-)25.80	228.7	2.10	(-)32.48	23.17	(-)0.52	13.98	(-)9.63	15.02
1993-94	3.09	(-)11.21	247.8	1.72	18.10	19.74	(-)14.80	10.99	(-)21.39	5.65
1994-95	12.34	299.35	274.7	6.20	260.47	35.82	81.46	17.99	60.69	34.46
1995-96	10.42	(-)15.56	295.8	4.86	(-)21.61	28.04	(-)21.72	13.08	(-)27.29	37.16
1996-97	3.61	(-)65.36	314.6	1.58	(-)67.49	14.54	(-)48.15	6.38	(-)51.22	24.76
1997-98	4.90	35.73	329.8	2.05	29.75	18.88	29.85	7.90	23.82	25.95
Total	64.00	375.51		39.73	263.65	267.93	54.08	176.72	(-)37.21	271.00
Mean	5.33	34.14		3.31	23.97	22.33	4.92	14.73	(-)3.38	22.58

Co-efficient correlation = 0.8775 Y = a+bx a = 3.31 a = 14.73

bx = 0.15 bx = (-) 0.31

Source: The Statement of Final Accounts of the above Institution.

Table 16.4 : Labour Cost and Output Karur Sarvodaya Sangh - Karur. (Whole sale Price Index - Base year 1986-87 - 138 points)

(Rs. in lakhs)

Year	*Labour Cost*	*Percentage of growth rate*	*Whole sale Price Index*	*Labour cost at the price level of 1986-87*	*Percentage of growth rate*	*Value of production*	*Percentage of growth rate*	*Production value at the price level of 1986-87*	*Percentage of growth rate*	*Share Percentage 5/9*
1	2	3	4	5	6	7	8	9	10	11
1986-87	32.33	-	138.0	32.23	-	92.66	-	92.66	-	34.78
1987-88	33.84	5.00	148.5	31.45	(-)2.42	87.94	5.09	81.72	(-)11.81	38.49
1988-89	39.52	16.78	154.2	35.37	12.46	58.89	(-)33.03	52.70	(-)35.51	67.12
1989-90	50.66	28.19	165.7	42.19	19.28	73.78	25.28	61.45	16.60	68.66
1990-91	51.20	1.07	182.7	38.67	(-)8.34	85.33	15.68	64.45	4.88	60.00
1991-92	56.11	9.59	207.8	37.26	(-)3.65	95.88	12.36	63.67	(-)1.21	58.52
1992-93	59.96	6.86	228.7	36.18	(-)2.90	101.67	6.04	61.35	(-)3.64	58.97
1993-94	59.66	(-)0.50	247.8	33.22	(-)8.18	102.11	0.43	56.87	(-)7.30	58.41
1994-95	63.69	6.75	274.7	32.00	(-)3.67	116.40	13.99	58.48	2.83	54.72
1995-96	100.27	57.43	295.8	46.78	46.19	156.39	34.36	72.96	24.76	64.12
1996-97	108.70	8.41	314.6	47.68	1.92	190.31	19.77	83.48	14.42	57.12
1997-98	107.91	(-)0.73	329.8	45.15	(-)5.31	173.72	(-)8.72	72.69	(-)12.93	62.11
Total	763.75	138.85		458.18	45.38	1335.08	80.94	822.48	(-)8.91	683.02
Mean	63.65	12.62		38.18	4.13	111.26	7.36	68.54	(-)0.81	56.92

Co-efficient correlation = 0.4436   Y = a+bx   a = 38.18, bx = 2.60   a = 68.54, bx = 2.47

Source : The Statement of Final Accounts of the above Institution.

increase. The increased wage from 1995-96 is only due to increase in the production wages as there is corresponding increase in the production. During the period under review the labour cost as per regression line increased at the rate of Rs.2,60 lakhs per annum. The salary and allowances to the staff which is a component of labour cost has no significant increase. The increased cost of labour is mainly due to engaging more labour for production activity.

Value of Production

In the case of VP in current price it has positive growth rate in the past two years and in deflated price levels it has negative growth rate in seven years. The mean averages of VP is negative. Reasons for this may be the following.

The main line of production of this institution Khadi and polyvastra. As stated earlier khadi has to complete with power loom, handloom, and the mill sector. Further, sale of Khadi in a reasonable volume is possible only during the rebate period of 90 days in a year. In order to keep the weavers and spinners in employment the production is to be carried out all through the year. Supervisory and administrative staff are to be given salary and other allowances even when there is no production. Hence there is no corresponding increase in VP in relation to increase in wages.

The mean average of cost of labour in current price is Rs.63.65 lakhs and at deflated prices Rs.38.18 lakhs. The mean average of the VP in current prices Rs.111.26 lakhs and in deflated prices Rs.68.54 lakhs. That is the relationship between these two variables is although positive it presents a poor relationship (r-0.4436).

Share of Percentage

The mean average share percentage of cost of labour and VP on both the prices is 56 per cent and it also tallies with, share of percentage of VP on labour cost which is 56.92. It may be pointed out that, out of five institutions under study this institution paid nearly 57 per cent of the value of production towards wage, the cost of labour.

TNSS

The particulars of cost of labour, VP, share of percentage etc of TNSS are furnished in table 16.5 for the period of twelve years.

Table 16.5 : Labour Cost and Output, Thiruchirapalli North Sarvodaya Sangh - Thiruchirapalli. (Wholesale Price Index - Base year 1986-87 - 138 points)

(Rs. in lakhs)

Year	*Labour Cost*	*Percentage of growth rate*	*Whole sale Price Index*	*Labour cost at the price level of 1986-87*	*Percentage of growth rate*	*Value of production*	*Percentage of growth rate*	*Production value at the price level of 1986-87*	*Percentage of growth rate*	*Share Percent-age 5/9*
1	2	3	4	5	6	7	8	9	10	11
1986-87	30.31	-	138.0	30.31	-	66.22	-	66.22	-	45.77
1987-88	34.31	12.60	148.5	31.88	4.65	79.42	19.93	73.80	11.45	42.98
1988-89	38.64	13.21	154.2	34.58	9.02	84.93	6.94	76.01	2.99	45.49
1989-90	35.07	(-)9.24	165.7	29.21	(-)15.53	57.24	(-)32.60	47.67	(-)37.28	61.28
1990-91	36.45	3.93	182.7	27.53	(-)5.75	76.52	33.68	57.80	21.25	47.63
1991-92	40.20	10.29	207.8	26.70	(-)3.01	83.42	9.02	55.40	(-) 4.15	48.19
1992-93	40.63	1.07	228.7	24.52	(-)8.16	70.01	(-)16.08	42.24	(-)23.75	58.05
1993-94	49.89	22.79	247.8	27.78	13.30	116.57	66.50	64.92	53.69	42.79
1994-95	56.20	12.65	274.7	28.23	1.62	99.61	(-)14.55	50.04	(-)22.92	56.41
1995-96	68.76	22.35	295.8	32.08	13.64	106.54	6.96	49.70	(-)0.68	65.43
1996-97	92.41	34.39	314.6	40.54	26.37	188.88	77.29	82.85	66.70	52.45
1997-98	105.92	14.62	329.8	44.32	9.32	229.12	21.30	95.87	15.72	46.23
Total	628.61	138.66		377.68	45.47	1258.48	178.39	762.52	83.02	612.70
Mean	52.38	12.61		31.47	4.13	104.87	16.22	63.54	7.55	51.06

Co-efficient correlation = 0.7400 Y = a+bx | a = 31.47, bx = 2.01 | a = 63.54, bx = 3.42

Source : The Statement of Final Accounts of the above Institution.

Table 16.6 : Labour Cost and Value of Production (Rs. in lakhs)

S. No.	*Name of the Institution*	*Labour cost mean average*	*VP mean average*	*Percentage of cost on VP*	*Rank*
1	GKVIPCT	52.26	171.29	30.50	II
2	MNSS	19.41	42.97	45.17	III
3	GSS	3.31	14.73	22.47	I
4	KSS	38.18	68.54	55.70	V
5	TNSS	31.47	63.54	49.51	IV
6	Total	144.63	361.07	40.05	
7	Average	28.92	72.24		

Cost of Labour and VP

Cost of labour in TNSS is fluctuating upto 1992-93 and afterwords it has shown a raising trend both in current and deflated prices. The mean average cost of labour in both the prices is positive as the mean averages of cost of labour in deflated prices is Rs.4.13 lakhs. The increased cost in real value is not appreciable with record to VP. There is no significant increase for a period of ten years except in the last two years 1996-97 and 1997-98. During the period the cost of labour appreciated at the rate of Rs.2.01 lakhs per annum. In the last two years the labour cost is also increased but it is productivity linked. In all the years salary and allowances to the staff members were stagnant which means major part of increased cost of labour is mainly due to increase in the production wages. The mean average of production at deflated price is Rs.7.55 lakhs and the labour cost is Rs. 4.13 lakhs. Therefore the labour component of VP is nearly 50 per cent and hence the mean averages is calculated as 51.06. Thus, the relationship between these two variables is highly positive r = 0.7400. This institution has also concentrated mainly on the production of Khadi and related activities and hence the wage component is high.

Labour Cost and Value of Production in KVI Institutions

The mean average of the cost of labour on VP of the five institution under study are give in table 16.6. Perusal of the table reveals that higher percentage of Labour Cost borne by KSS and the lowest labour cost offered by G.S.S. It is clear that the institution which undertake khadi as the main activity has to pay more wages. The three institutions namely KSS MNSS and TNSS have paid 55.70 per cent, 45.17 per cent and 49.51 per cent respectively towards the cost of labour on total value of production. Now it is proved once again that khadi activities are labour oriented and hence it involves higher labour cost. The major part of production value goes to workers as wages.

The other two institutions namely GKVIPCT and GSS have diversified their activities and they undertake more VI activities than Khadi. Comparing to GKVIPCT, GSS undertake very little khadi activity and hence the wage component is 22.47 per cent and GKVIPCT paid 30.50 per cent towards labour cost as it has more khadi activity than GSS.

It is proved that labour input on khadi activity is nearly 50 per cent on total value of production and for Village Industries activities, it is around 25 per cent.

Further Research Suggested

The present exercise total labour cost of Direct labour, Indirect labour, Part-time labour, and the cost of salary for the administrative staff, managers etc are studied. Further study may be undertaken micro level taking the cost of direct labour only.

REFERENCES

1. Pratibha Goyal: *Preface Labour Welfare and Job Satisfication*, Deep and Deep Publication, New Delhi - 1995. Front page.
2. Sanjib Roy : "A review on Cost of Labour and Labour Productivity in Indian Tea Industry", *The Management Accountant*, Calcutta. Vol.32, No. 9 September 1997, pp. 702-704
3. Michael. P. Todaro : *Economic Development*, Longman Publishing, New York - 1994. pp. 223-224.
4. Padmanabhan, V.: "KVI Sector and the Unemployment Scenario", *Khadi Gramodyog*, Mumbai, vol. XXXVII, No.1, October, 1990, p.13
5. Dewett, K.K., Varma, J.D., and Sharma, M.L.: *Indian Economics*, Sultan Chand & Company Ltd., Delhi - 1998. p. 465.
6. Hansra, B.S., and Gangadrappa, N.R., : "Youth As Hunger Fighter", *Intensive Agriculture*, September - October, 1999, p. 5.
7. Rajan, V. : "Gandhiji on Employment and Education in India", *Khadi Gramodyog*, Mumbai, Vol.XXXI, No.1, October, 1994, p. 28.
8. Rama Rao, A. : "Role of Khadi and Village Industries and Right to Work", *Khadi Gramodyog*, Mumbai, Vol.XXXVII, No.1, October,1990, p. 32.
9. Padmanabhan,V. : "KVI Sector and The Unemployment Scenario", *Khadi Gramodyog*, Mumbai, Vol. XXXVII, No. 1, October,1990, p. 13.

10. Sen, K.K., *Rural Industrialisation in India*, Sultan Chand and Company, New Delhi, 1996, p. 109.
11. Rajan,V., *op. cit.,* p. 29.
12. Jasvir Singh : "Poverty Human Rights and Minimum Wages", *Khadi Gramodygo*, Mumbai, Vol-XXXXIV, No.2, Nov-Dec, 1997, and Jan. 1998, p. 125.
13. Lallan Prasad and A.M. Bannerjee : *Management of Human Resources*, Sterling Publishers Private Limited, New Delhi, 1994, p. 237.
14. Prasanna Chandra : *Projects Planning Analysis Selection Implementation and Review*, Tata McGraw Hill Publishing Company Limited, New Delhi, pp. 104-106.

17

Performance of Tamil Nadu Industrial Cooperative Bank Limited, Chennai

A Study

K. RAJA ALIAS PRANMALAI AND S. RAMASAMY

Introduction

After the British rule in India, cottage and small scale industries had gradually deteriorated. These industries were staggering for want of adequate finance, raw materials and technical guidance and marketing facilities. In order to solve these problems, the Govt of India and the State Government have taken positive measures in the establishment of Cottage and Small Scale Industries on co-operative lines which play a key role in the development of national economy. They create direct and subsidiary occupation to a sizable proportion of our rural and urban population.

The Industries Commission in 1918 suggested the importance of giving a distinctly cooperative bias to cottage and small-scale industries. Again the Royal Commission on Agriculture in 1929 suggested the organization of village artisans on a cooperative basis for credit, raw materials and marketing. The Industrial Policy Resolution of 1948 and 1956 advocated the development of cottage and small-scale industries on cooperative lines. The suggestions given by the commissions and the industrial policy resolution were taken into consideration and cottage and small scale industries have been organized in cooperative lines, because in India, cooperatives play a vital role in rural transformation in the form of socio-economic and political arena. The industrial cooperatives not only provide employment and income but also extend social responsibility to masses; hence the industrial co-operatives came to existence.

Industrial Cooperative Bank in India

The industrial cooperatives were established first in France. Later they spread over the world. In India, the industrial cooperatives have been organised for weaver's, artisans, coir producers etc. Though, District Central Cooperative Banks have been providing loan to industrial co-operative societies, there was no specific financing institution to lend finance to industrial co-operatives in the beginning in all states. Above all the District Central Co-operative Banks were unable to cater to the credit needs of the Industrial co-operative societies. Hence, The Government of India decided to establish industrial cooperative bank in order to meet the credit requirement of Industrial co-operative society; therefore a separate, organised industrial cooperative bank was established in some states like Karnataka, Rajasthan and Tamil Nadu.

The Japanese delegation on small-scale industries (1959) also had pointed out that agricultural and industrial banks had their respective features and the existing central cooperative bank's interest was lend credit to agricultural cooperatives than to industrial cooperatives. They recommended the promoting of state cooperative banks for industrial cooperatives, which would perform the functions of providing required short term and long term funds to the industrial cooperatives through the banks' head and branch offices.

Statement of the Problem

Cooperative banks are concentrating mainly on agricultural credit in India through their well-established rural credit banks. But the District Central Cooperative Banks are far from satisfactory in providing credit to non-agricultural activities. Hence, the Industrial Cooperative Bank has been entrusted the responsibility of lending credit to cottage and small-scale industries organised on co-operative line in India. Accordingly co-operatives in Tamil Nadu were transferred to the Department of Industries and Commerce in 1956. TAICO Bank the short form of Tamil Nadu Industrial Co-operative Bank was registered on 13-9-1961 and started functioning from November 1962.

After the introduction of new economic policy and globalisation the industrial cooperative banks have been facing a number of problems with regard to financial, operational and managerial aspects. Since industrial cooperative bank is the financing agency for the industrial cooperative society, it is highly relevant to have a probe into the performance of industrial cooperative bank in relation to development of industrial cooperatives. Hence, TAICO Bank, Chennai was identified and selected for the study.

Objectives of the Study

The specific objectives of the study are :

(a) To analyse the performance of the Bank and
(b) To find out the problems of the bank and suggest suitable measures for the effective functioning of the bank.

Fig. 17.1 : Performance of TAICO Bank from 1995-96 to 1999-2000

Year	*Member (Nos)*	*Share capital Rs. in lakhs*	*Deposits Rs. in lakhs*	*Borrowings Rs. in lakhs*	*Reserve Fund Rs. in lakhs*	*Working capital Rs. in lakhs*	*Recovery Rs. in lakhs*	*Profits Rs. in lakhs*
1995-96	482	409.17	2634.06	563.97	541.99	15512.02	112.91	22.59
1996-97	476	412.03	3211.25	428.44	605.02	10343.87	180.08	21.14
		(0.70)	-21.91	(-24.03)	-11.63	(-33.31)		
1997-98	479	415.96	2063.13	367.65	761.58	17420.35	202.32	-105.97
		-0.95	-35.75	(-14.19)	-25.87	-68.41		
1998-99	480	416.08	3290.29	309.42	975.91	17975.72	251.04	-157.26
		-0.03	-59.48	(-15.84)	-28.14	-3.18		
1999-2000	489	414.71	4467.53	226.91	1331.06	12447.26	429.59	-273.31
		(-0.33)	-35.78	(-26.67)	-36.04	(-30.75)		

Figures in paranthesis show the growth rate.
Source : Annual and Audit reports of TAICO bank from 1995 to 2000.

Method of Data Collection

Case study method had been adopted for this study. Both primary and secondary sources of data were collected and used. For data collection a well structured and pre-tested schedule was used. The data were collected from TAICO bank officials at different levels. Annual reports and audit reports of the bank were referred to elicit data on the performance of the bank.

The collected data were analysed systematically by employing the statistical tools like percentage, growth rate and ratio analysis. The study covers a period of five years from 1995-96 to 1999-2000.

Major Findings of the Study

The following are identified as major outcome from the analysis of the data :

(1) Industrial cooperatives, State Government, SSI and individuals are the members of industrial cooperative bank.
(2) The cooperative societies were the highest membership contributors (453) in 1995-96 than other members like state government, Small-scale industries and individuals.
(3) There was no substantial growth in the membership position of the bank due to apathy of sick industrial cooperatives and withdrawal of membership during the study period.
(4) The share capital position of the TAICO bank shows an increasing trend from 1995-96 to 1998-99 and it has come down in the year 1999-2000 and registered a negative growth rate of -0.33 per cent.
(5) The growth rate of reserve fund of the bank was the highest (36.04 per cent) in 1999-2000 and the lowest (11.63 per cent) in 1996-97.
(6) The bank is maintaining current deposit, savings bank deposit and fixed deposit accounts. The composition of deposits growth rate of bank has been fluctuating over the study period, it has the highest deposit growth rate of 59.48 per cent in 1998-99 the lowest of 21.91 per cent during 1996-97.
(7) TAICO bank borrowed funds from NABARD and Tamil Nadu Backward Class Economic Development Corporation (TABCEDCO). But the borrowing amount had been gradually decreasing from Rs. 563.97 lakhs in 1995-96 to Rs. 226.91 lakhs in 1999-2000.
(8) The TAICO bank earned a profit of Rs. 22.59 lakhs and Rs. 21.14 lakhs in 1995-96 and 1996-97 respectively. During the remaining three years it incurred a loss of Rs. 273.31 lakhs in 1999-2000.
(9) The bank shows poor recovery performance during the study period.
(10) The bank has 22 branches all over the state. The number of branches are more or less constant during the period of study. The reason for it are competitive environment and lack of professionalisation of management which are the causes for

TAICO banks' not showing better performance. So these are the main hindrances for the development of TAICO bank in Tamil Nadu.

Suggestions

Based on the findings of the study the following are the suggestions for the effective performance of industrial co-operative bank in India :

(1) The state industrial cooperative bank may provide appropriate training for employees of industrial cooperative bank.
(2) The present study revealed that there was no proper auditing and accounting done before 1997 in some branches. Therefore, proper and systematic auditing should be done every year in order to evaluate the realistic performance of the bank.
(3) Need oriented policy support must be extended by both Central and State Government for the development of industrial cooperatives.
(4) In order to activate the effective functioning of industrial cooperative bank, it has to be merged with concerned district central cooperative banks by establishing a separate department exclusively for lending credit to industrial cooperatives and self-help groups.

Conclusion

The overall performance of the Tamil Nadu Industrial Cooperative Bank was not satisfactory. It has to strengthen its operational efficiency in order to compete with the multinational financing institutions in the years to come.

REFERENCES

Annual and Audit Reports of TAICO Bank from 1995-96 to 1999-2000.

Desai, S.S.M.; *Rural Banking in India,* Himalaya Publishing House "Ramdoot", Dr. Bhalerao Marg (Kelewad) Girgaon, Bombay, 1986.

Mamoria, C.B.; *Agricultural Problems of India*, Kitab Mahal, 15, Thronhill Road, Allahabad.

Mathur, Dr. B.S.; *Co-operation in India*, Sahitya Bhavan, Hospital Road, Agra, 1991.

18

Production and Process of Vegetable Oils

K. MURUGESAN

Most vegetable oils are obtained from beans or seeds, which generally furnish two valuable commodities – an oil and a protein-rich meal. Seed extraction is achieved by pressing and/or by solvent extraction. Using figures for 2000-01, world average oil yields are: soybean (18.3%); coconut (38.6 %); sunflower (40.9%); groundnut (40.3 %); cottonseed (15.1%); average for all oilseeds (25.8%). In addition, yields from palm fruit (45-50%), olive (25-30%) and corn (about 5%) are as indicated.

Some oils, such as virgin olive oil, are used without further treatment but most are refined in some measure before use. The refining processes remove undesirable materials (phospholipids, monoacylglycerols, diacylglycerols, free acids, colour and pigments, oxidized materials, flavour components, trace metals and sulfur compounds) but may also remove valuable minor components which are antioxidants and vitamins such as carotenes and tocopherols. These processes must therefore be designed to maximize the first and to minimize the second. Some of the useful minor components can be recovered from side streams to give valuable products such as phospholipids, free acids, tocopherols, carotenes, sterols and squalene.

With only a limited number of oils and fats available on a commercial scale, it is not surprising that these are sometimes inadequate to meet the physical, nutritional, and chemical properties required for use in food products. Over a century or more, lipid technologists have designed and used procedures for overcoming the limitations of a restricted range of natural products. In particular, they have sought to modify the fatty acid composition of their lipids, knowing that such changes will influence the physical, nutritional, and chemical properties.

Methods of changing fatty acid composition and physical, nutriztional and chemical properties thereby

Technological Solutions

Blending
Distillation
Fractionation
Hydrogenation
Interesterification with chemical catalysts
Interesterification with specific lipases
Enzymic enhancement

Biological Solutions

Domestication of wild crops
Oils modified by conventional seed breeding
Oils modified by (intra-species) genetic engineering
Lipids from unconventional sources (micro-organisms)

The procedures most relevant are fractionation, hydrogenation and modification of fatty acid composition, either by conventional seed breeding or by genetic engineering. World production of oils and fats – currently about 117 million tones per annum – comes from vegetable and animal sources. Oil World publication* recognize 17 commodity oils, of which four are of animal origin. The remainder are from vegetable sources.

Of the total production of oils and fats, about 80 per cent is used for food purposes 6 per cent is used in animal feed, and the remaining 14 per cent provides the basis of the oleochemical industry. Within the sources of vegetable oils it is useful to distinguish three different types:

- *Byproducts:* Cotton and corn are grown primarily for fibre and for cereal respectively and the oil is a byproduct. Soybean can also be included in this category because it yields two products—oil and meal–which represent approximately 18 per cent and 79 per cent respectively of the dried bean. The demand for soybeans is driven sometimes by one of these and sometimes by the other. It could also be argued that peanuts (groundnuts) should also be included, since only about one half of the crop is crushed (for oil and meal) and the rest is consumed as nuts.

- *Tree crops:* Palm, palmkemel, coconut and olive oils are obtained from trees that have to be planted and mature before they give a useful crop. Once this stage is reached, the trees continue to provide crops for 25-30 years, in the case of palm, and longer than that for olive. These crops cannot be changed on a yearly basis.
- *Annual crops:* The third category are annual crops such as rape, sun-flower and !inseed. Appropriate decisions have to be made annually by the farmer or planter concerning which crops to grow. The choice is usually between oilseed crops and cereals, and the decision is based on agricultural and economic factors.

Another distinction that is sometimes made between oilseed crops

Table 18.1 : Production, exports and imports (mil!ion tones) of 10 oilseeds and of 17 oils and in selected countries in 2000-01

		Oilseeds			*Oils and fats*		
	*Population**	*Production*	*Exports*	*Imports*	*Production*	*Exports*	*Imports*
World	6133	306.9	64.7	64.7	117.1	37.7	37.7
Malaysia	23	3.4	-	0.7	13.6	11.5	0.4
Argentina	37	29.6	5.9	-	5.3	4.5	-
Canada	31	10.7	6.3	0.8	2.2	1.1	0.4
Australia	19	2.9	1.8	-	0.9	0.5	0.2
US	286	85.1	28.2	0.8	15.7	2.9	1.9
Brazil	173	38.7	12.8	0.6	5.5	1.4	0.3
Indonesia	215	5.1	-	1.5	8.9	5.6	-
China	1263	47.8	0.9	14.4	15.8	0.2	2.9
India	1025	20.8	0.2	-	6.7	0.2	5.9
EU-15	377	14.6	0.7	20.5	15.2	2.6	5.2

* Million

and those vegetable oils which come from the endosperm (soft fleshy fruit). Palm and olive belong to this category.

Most of the crops are produced annually at harvest time, which comes late in the calendar year in the northern hemisphere and early in the calendar year in the southern hemisphere. However, some equatorial crops like palm and coconut are harvested through all the twelve months of the year, though there is some minor seasonal variation in quantity.

In discussing the trade in oilseed, oils and fats, and oil meals in geographical terms it is useful to divide countries/regions into four categories. These are discussed below and illustrated in Table 18.1.

- Countries with small populations that produce large amounts of oilseeds/oils and fats are the world's largest exporters of these commodities and dominate world trade. Examples include Malaysia, Argentina, Canada and Australia.
- Countries with large populations that produce large amounts of oilseeds/oils and fats. These countries need to feed their own large populations but are still significant exporters. Examples are the US, Brazil and Indonesia.
- Countries with very large populations which, despite local production, are still major importers. China and India and other highly populated countries in Asia belong to this category.

Table 18.2 : Annual average production of 17 oils and fats in selected five-year periods from 1976-80 with forecasts up to 2016-20

	1976-80	*1986-90*	*1996-2000*	*2006-10*	*2016-20*
World total	52.65	75.66	105.06	165.65	184.77
Soybean oil	11.23	15.28	23.14	33.60	41.12
Cottonseed oil	2.83	3.64	4.00	5.35	6.51
Groundnut oil	3.01	3.70	4.55	5.72	6.38
Sunflower seed oil	4.21	7.25	9.11	12.43	16.97
Rapeseed oil	3.01	7.51	12.64	17.72	22.69
Sesame seed oil	0.51	0.64	0.70	0.86	0.96
Corn oil	0.83	1.35	1.91	2.49	3.16
Olive oil	1.68	1.80	2.47	2.75	2.98
Palm oil	3.69	9.22	18.72	31.43	43.36
Palmkernel oil	0.46	1.21	2.34	3.84	5.28
Coconut oil	2.85	3.07	3.01	3.70	4.55
Butter	5.60	6.35	5.81	6.93	7.99
Lard	4.25	5.17	6.38	7.93	9.14
Fist oil	1.13	1.53	1.25	1.18	11.59
Linseed oil	0.79	0.73	0.70	0.81	0.97
Castor seed oil	0.32	0.40	0.46	0.71	0.78
Tallow	6.24	6.79	7.85	10.06	10.76

- Finally there are countries/regions which are essentially trades. They produce, consume, import, and export these commodities, EU-15 is the biggest example but Hong Kong (as was) and Singapore, by virture of their geographical closeness to the world's largest importer (China) and exporter (Malaysia), are also significant traders.

Table 17.2 shows the annual average production of 17 oils and fats for selected five-year periods from 1976-80 with forecasts up to 2016-20 taken from a revised Oil World publication in 2002. That is a period of forty years. There has been a considerable increase in oil and fat production during that time from 53 million tonnes in 1976-80 to 105 million tonnes in 1996-2000 with 185 million tonnes expected in 20 years' time.

The production levels of virtually all the commodities have increased during the past 20 years and further increases are expected in the coming years.

Typical among oils which have lost market share over the past twenty years are cottonseed oil, which has fallen from 5.4 to 3.8 per cent , groundnut oil (from 5.7 to 4.3 per cent), and olive oil (from 3.2 to 2.3 per cent), despite the increase in production shown in Table 18.2.

Table 18.3 : Four major vegetable oils as per cent of total oil and fat production

	1976-80	1986-90	1996-2000	2006-10	2016-20
Soybean oil	21.3	20.2	22.0	22.9	20.2
Palm and pko*	7.9	13.8	20.0	24.0	26.3
Rapeseed oil	5.7	9.9	12.0	12.1	12.3
Sunflower seed oil	8.0	9.6	8.7	8.5	9.2

* Palmkernel oil

Annual production of oils and fats in 2000-01 is expected to be about 117 million tonnes. Given an average price range of $300-500 per tonne, this indicates a total value of $35-60 billion for the year's oils and fats production.

Following table attention is focused on the five years 1996-97 to 2000-01 to show the most recent trends. These double dates are 'harvest years'. The earlier date relates to the harvest of the northern hemisphere and the later figure to that of the southern hemisphere. Oils and fats come from oilseeds, fruits, and from animal sources and

Table gives figures for 10 oilseeds. Most of the seed is crushed, but some is held back as seed for planting and some is used directly for animal feed or human food. Crushing produces oil and meal. The proportion of these varies slightly from year to year, depending on the relative amounts of the various oilseeds with their differing levels of oil.

Table 18.4 : Global production of 10 oilseeds and of oil and meal derived from these (million tonnes) during the five-year period 1996-97 to 2000-01

	1996-97	1997-98	1998-99	1999-2000	2000-01
Production	259.79	285.95	295.38	302.84	306.2
Crushing	222.60	233.36	242.34	251.99	59.27
Oil	57.39	59.73	61.78	65.30	66.80
Meal	149.96	158.63	165.58	171.46	177.63

Source : Mielke 2001

Table 18.5 : Production (million tonnes) of 12 vegetable oils during the five-year period 1996-97 to 2000-01

	1996-97	1997-98	1998-99	1999-2000	2000-01
Soybean	20.96	23.18	24.60	25.30	26.66
Palm	17.57	17.10	19.36	21.26	23.38
Rapeseed	11.48	12.19	12.56	14.30	14.15
Sunflower seed	9.11	8.44	9.28	9.57	8.87
Groundnut	4.61	4.36	4.78	4.53	4.86
Cottonseed	4.06	4.13	3.89	3.92	3.89
Coconut	3.14	3.37	2.35	3.09	3.43
Palmkernel	2.19	2.20	2.43	2.63	2.89
Olive	2.77	2.62	2.54	2.35	2.56
Corn	1.85	1.89	1.92	2.00	2.03
Sesame	0.72	0.74	0.72	0.73	0.78
Linseed	0.67	0.68	0.73	0.74	0.72

Source : Mielke 2001.

Table 18.6 : Production, disappearance, export and imports (million tonnes) of 17 oils and fats during the five-year period 1996-97 to 2000-01

	1996-97	*1997-98*	*1998-99*	*1999-2000*	*2000-01*
Production	100.14	102.03	107.51	113.44	117.12
Disappearance	99.82	102.37	106.61	112.24	117.54
Per person (kg)	17.1	17.3	17.8	18.5	19.2
Exports	32.04	33.11	34.08	35.10	37.69
Imports	31.40	33.25	33.76	35.42	37.67

Source : Mielke 2001

It should be explained that 'disappearance' is a technical term. Applied to a country/region for a particular year, it is the sum of local production and imports with deduction of exports and allowance for changes in stocks during the year in question. It includes human consumption, animal feed, industrial consumption, and waste, and cannot be equated directly with dietary intake. Disappearance per person is expressed in kg/year and is available on a world basis or for individual countries/regions. Disappearance per person has shown a steady rise over many years. In the years between 1996-97 and 2000-01, it has risen 12 per cent from 17.1 to 19.2 kg/year. Exports and imports are at virtually the same level and correspond to 31-32 per cent of total production. The balance is used in the country where it is produced.

Table 18.7 : Predicted total (million tonnes) and per capita consumption (kg per annum) of oils and fats on a global basis and for selected countries/regions throughout the century

	2000	2020	2040	2060	2080	2100
Total	114	219	364	542	736	971
Vegetable oils	92	190	328	498	685	914
Populations (billions)	6.08	7.90	9.23	9.99	10.18	10.35
Consumption per person						
World	19	28	39	54	72	94
US	52	68	85	100	113	124
EU-15	47	62	77	90	102	112
China	13	28	49	74	99	122
India	12	21	33	48	66	84

Source: Fry 2001.

James Fry of LMC International (Oxford and New York) has examined changes in the production and demand for oils and fats in the past quarter century (1976-2000) and made projections for the twenty-first century (Fry 2001). Between 1976 and 2000, consumption in oils and fats increased at an average rate of 3.7 per cent equivalent to a doubling every 20 years or so. For animal and marine fats, the increase was only 1.4 per cent and for vegetable oils 4.5 per cent. The four major oils have increased at average rates of 8.3 per cent for palm oil, 7.3 per cent for rapeseed oil, 4.5 per cent for sunflower oil, and 4.1 per cent for soybean oil. These increases results from a combination of higher yields and of larger areas devoted to their production. The very large increase in palm oil has come mainly from the increase in area, and only to a minor extent from a rise in yield, while the three oilseed crops show significant increases in yield as well as in area under cultivation.

Extrapolation of figures for the past 40 years over the next 100 produces ridiculous conclusions with population increasing six fold to 36 billion, consumption per person of oils and fats increasing to a world average of 110 kilos per annum, and world production of 4 billion tonnes in 2100. More reasonably, it is now widely accepted that population will level out half-way through the century at around 10 billion, and Fry has made other assumptions about growth in personal GDP and the link between income and fat consumption. On this basis, he has calculated the production of total oils and fats and of vegetable oils and disappearance on a world basis.

REFERENCES

Gunstone, F.D. (1998) Movements towards tailor-made fats. *Prog. Lipid Res.*, 37, 277-305.

Gunstone, F.D. (2000) Composition and properties of edible oils, in *Edible Oil* Processing (eds W.Hamm and R.J.Hamilton), Sheffield Academic Press, Sheffield, pp.1-33.

Gunstone, F.D. (2001) Oilseed crops with modified fatty acid composition. *J.Oleo Sci.*, 50, 269-279.

Gunstone, F.D. and Hamiton, R.J.(eds) (2001) *Oleochemical Manufacture and Applications,* Sheffield Academic Press, Sheffield.

Hamm, W. (2001) Regional differences in edible oil processing procedures. 1. Seed crusing and extraction, oil movements, and degumming. 2. Refining, oil modification, and formulation. Lipid Tech.

Mielke, T. (ed) (2001) *Oil World Annual 2001,* ISTA Mielke GmgH, Hamburg, Germany.

Mielke, T. (ed) (2002) *The Revised Oil World 2020,* ISTA Mielke GmbH, Hamburg, Germany.

19

Decorticating Industries in Theni District

A Study

S. Maria John

Growth of the Small Scale Industries in India is a significant feature of the Indian Economy. The Small Scale Sector covers wide range of activities. It is also playing a pivotal role in employment generation with low capital investment. At present it has provided employment opportunities to around 18 million people. The Government of India, recognising the importance and role of rural industries, has been allocating large amounts during all the plan periods.

Table 19.1 provides the plan outlays during the plan periods (vide Table 19.1). In India Small Scale Industries include traditional and modern small industries, cottage industries, tiny units, business and industry related services etc. Consequent to the provisions during the plan periods, there has been tremendous growth of Small and Rural Industries (vide Table 19.2).

Cottage Industries as feeder units to other industrial units, are mostly managed by artisans and skilled craftsman and are involved in traditional activities such as agriculture, khadi, handlooms, handicrafts, etc. These are generally associated with part time or full time occupations in rural and semi urban areas utilizing locally available resources and or human skill.

Tiny units are the enterprises having an investment limit of less than 5 lakhs, whereas ancillary units have Rs.75 lakhs. These ancillary units are engaged in manufacturing parts, components, sub assemblies, toolings or intermediaries rendering services to one or more industrial units. These also serve as supporting units to large industries. The small and tiny units account for 35 per cent of the gross value of the output in the manufacturing sector, about 80 per cent of the total industrial employment and about 40 per cent of the total exports of the country.

Table 19.1 : Plan outlays for Rural Industrialisation

Sl. No.	*Plan Period*	*Outlays Rs. In Crores*	*Cumulative Percentage*
1	First Plan	42	0.34
2	Second Plan	187	1.86
3	Third Plan	241	3.81
4	Annual Plan	126	4.83
5	Fourth Plan	293	7.20
6	Fifth Plan	592	11.99
7	Sixth Plan	1780	26.41
8	Seventh Plan	2753	48.7
9	Eighth Plan	6334	100
	Growth rate in percentage	15081	-

Growth rate is calculated as yt/yo × 100

Service establishments are units involved in all industry related service and business enterprises, irrespective of location with recognised potential for generating employment. The investment ceilings correspond to those of tiny units.

The Cottage Industries are more or less house hold industries depending on local resources catering only to a limited local market. These industries may be classified into :

(1) Part-time rural cottage industries,
(2) Whole-time rural industries, and
(3) Urban Cottage Industries.

The part-time rural cottage industries cover all such industries which provide supplementary occupation to agriculturists and which are mostly processing industries, agro based industries, fruits and vegetable preservation and utilisation, Handloom Weaving, Tadi, palm gur Jaggary making and basket and rope making etc.

This study relates in general to groundnut industries which are agro-based processing industries. Groundnut is used in two types of village industries. They are.

(1) Groundnut decorticating industries and
(2) Oil industries

In a decorticating industry groundnut is processed, i.e., the outer shell or covering is removed. This decortication is done by machines by employing some persons in the premises of the entrepreneur. The other activities included in processing groundnut are drying, storing, packing etc. This processed kernel is sold to the following: (vide Table 19.3).

Table 19.2 : Growth of Small and Rural Industries (1980-81 to 1998-99)

Period	*No. of Units (in Lakhs)*	*Production (Rs. in Crores)*	*Employment (Inlakhs)*	*Exports (Rs.in Crores)*
1980-81	4.48	28060	71.	1643
1984-85	8.50	50520	90.	2580
1988-89	11.59	106400	113.	5490
1992-93	22.35	209300	134.	17785
1996-97	28.57	412636	160.	39249
1998-99	31.21	538357	175.2	57488

Table 19.3 : Pattern of Distribution of Processed Nut by Entrepreneurs

Sl.No.	*Category*	*Percentage*
1	Small business people	16
2	Other business people	38
3	Wholesalers	14
4	Oil industries direct cottage	15
5	Large oil units-own	17

(1) Small business people i.e., those who carry on cottage business at their homes.
(2) Other business people i.e., those who carry on provision type of business.
(3) Wholesalers who deal only in kernel business and
(4) Sent to oil industries (Cottage) and
(5) Large Oil Units

Oil industries indulge in extracting oil from the processed kernel. These industries take oil not only from groundnut but also from other types of Dhals and Seeds. The reason behind this is that of inconsistency in supply of groundnut to these entrepreneur. They get cake too which is sold separately.

Oil industries are of two types, they are :

(1) Oil industries carrying on business at large scale, and
(2) Oil industries which are carried on at very small scale

Table 19.4 : Factories and Industries Located in Theni District

Sl. No.	*Category*	*Percentage*
1	Registered Working Factories	301
2	Large Scale Industries	18
3	Medium Scale Industries	12
4	Small Scale Industries	582
5	Cottage Industries	150
6	Unregistered Cottage Units	NA

i.e. this type of industries are run either at the own residence of the entrepreneur or at a small hired place and employing a very few workers. They use one or two machines. These people extract oil from various dhals and nuts.

This research was carried on in Aundipatti Taluk (Theni District–Tamil Nadu) which consists of many types of industries (vide Table 19.4) and nearly 20 groundnut industries. These industries comprise both decorticating and oil industries. Theni District has 5 Taluks Viz., Aundipatti, Bodinayakanur, Uthamapalayam, Periyakulam and Theni.

In all the Taluks there has been groundnut production every year. During some years the production in one Taluk exceeds the production of the other Taluk. Among all the Taluks, the production of groundnut in Aundipatti Taluk, often exceeds the production of other Taluks, has three significance viz.

(a) Large production in quantity,
(b) Large production in quality (size of the nut), and
(c) More oil content.

The nature of the soil of Aundipatti and the climatic conditions have proved more productivity of groundnut in the locality. As there is more demand for the groundnut cultivated in and around Aundipatti Taluk, this area has been selected for the study. On the basis of the maximum turnover of groundnut in the industries of the sample area, 10 industries (5 decorticating industries and 5 oil industries) were selected and a survey has proved that the sample respondents have been facing many problems in connection with handling of the kernel.

The very object of the study is to probe into the various problems (both economical and technological) faced by the respondents and to suggest to possible recommendations that require immediate action.

Findings of the study

Shortage of Raw materials

The cottage worker suffers from acute shortage of raw material. The groundnut industry is wholly dependent upon the supply of raw groundnut. The groundnut growers are unable to supply the nut, through out the year, to the industries, as this crop is seasonal. Hence the shortage of raw groundnut is always felt. In the study area there are two types of industries viz.

(a) Industries at large scale of operation
(b) Industries at low scale of operations.

The industries which indulge in huge business operations are rightly categorised as healthy business enterprises. They buy more raw materials, produce more, sell more and enjoy more. They also procure and hoard groundnut in bulk and operate the market. The average industries and low scale operating industries have to depend largely on the market operators. They fix the price of the groundnut (raw materials) and act as middlemen in the field. Thus the artisan does not get enough of what he wants, what he gets is of poor quality and that too has to be bought at higher price.

Lack of Credit and Finance

The financial disability of small artisans is beyond doubt. Their financial needs consists of the purchase of raw materials, working expenses and accommodation between production & sale of the products. The internal sources are quite inadequate. This leads to instability of their profits which deters banks from giving unsecured loans. Their requirements are met by village money lenders who charge usurious rate of interest. The total amount of loan granted to them by the commercial banks forms a very small part of the total loans to the industry.

Low Level of Technology and Skill

The development of the village and small scale industries is hampered by the present low level of technology and shortage of trained and experienced supervisory personnel. So that the methods and art of production technique especially the producers for want of information, know very little about modern technologies which have revolutionised production in small units in advanced countries. There is little research and development in this field in the country.

Competition from Large Scale Industries

Large scale industries, organised as they are on modern lines, using latest production technology and having access to many facilities can easily outsell the small producers. The small producers cannot therefore, stand up against them in the market.

Sickness and Inefficiency

Quite a large proportion of small industries has fallen sick. Their number run into lakhs. At present as many as 2.96 lakhs units are sick. This is exclusive over a lakh sick units which are not traceable or are not in existence. The reason for such sickness is that in many of the units 45 per cent to 60 per cent of its capacity remains unutilised. The reason may be incompetent manager, improper location, insufficient technology, skill, inadequate infrastructure facilities etc.

Inadequate Cost Analysis

Inadequate product-cost analysis blinds entrepreneurs to the losses incurred by adding new products willy-nilly. As the sample members deal with many products viz. coconut, neem seed, gingely seed etc. they could not calculate the cost per product. Usually, there are one or more products or product lines that should be dropped.

Another common failing is gearing the operations to the income statement and ignoring the other financial statements. Lack of concern with cash flow and the productivity of capital employed can be fatal to the small company that is on its own. Entrepreneurs can make better use of the funds which they already have by making use of financial statements rather than seeking for new funds. Thus entrepreneurs need to realise that the surest test of their business success is sufficient and profits growing from year to year.

Cost of Electricity

Separation of oil and cake from the concerned raw materials requires the use of machineries. Machines, now-a-days are not operated by men, but by electricity. The cottage entrepreneur, who uses machineries, are charged the commercial rate (Rs.3.20 per unit) by the electricity boards. This is a great burden to these small entrepreneurs which prevent their growth and expansion.

Collection of Debts

A businessman cannot depend only on cash sales. He has to depend on credit sales too. Credit sales is profitable as well as a risky affair. Most of the entrepreneurs face the problem of debt collection. It has been proved that there has been an average of 25 per cent bad debts on credit sales which is made to small house hold businessmen this occurrence of bad debts is due to the downfall of small cottage units, diversification of business (change of business) loss in business, family commitments, etc.

No business can operate without inventories. It needs protection. Guarding inventory thus becomes essential and forms strength to the unit.

Inventory comes in various forms such as Supplies, Raw materials, Goods in process of manufacture, Finished goods and Floor stock (display).

It is always prudent to guard inventory as well as the inventories cost money in several ways.

Groundnut occupies a vast floor area. So a business man has to allocate a major portion of the industry for keeping the raw groundnut, semi-finished and finished stock. Maintenance of the whole area for keeping of the goods results ultimately in high cost.

Groundnut production is purely seasonal. So a large volume of raw groundnut is to be preserved till it is used in the process of production. The harvesting season lasts just for 2 months only. So the businessmen dealing in groundnut have to invest a lot in procuring raw groundnut. As, with in a short period, their raw groundnut has to be procured for storing, the businessmen are unable to generate the fund from their own business. Hence they borrow. Thus by this process money is tied up. This tie up money causes payment of interest.

Raw groundnut has to be stored for a very long time in the factory. So risk is more in preservation. So to get rid of from the risk, the entire stock is insured. Insurance in this respect is considered to be costly as premium is paid on the basis of the area of storage.

Storage is done in large areas. Hence it is bound to pay property tax on them. Cost of production from pilferage and weather, pests and insects also cause damage. So to destroy them some cost is incurred.

Marketing Problem

Marketing the groundnut oil is the major problem faced by the small and large entrepreneurs. The sample members are of the opinion that, if at all they could sell one kilogram of groundnut oil atleast for Rs.40, it will be of benefit to them. At this situation, it is very difficult, if not impossible, to sell them at this required price. It is due to the Globalisation policy of the government (bilateral agreement). As the price of groundnut oil is more, consequently the demand decreases. Another reason for such a fall in demand for this oil is that of the import of palmoline (Palmoil) by the government even at Rs.21 per litre. So the middle income group as well as the people below and at poverty line switch on to the substitute. At present the price of Gingely oil has also fallen down to a certain extent.

Suggestions

There are many problems which stand as an obstacle on the improvement of groundnut industry. In this study the problems with regard to inventories are mostly highlighted and some suggestions for optimising the inventory have been made.

The businessmen can opt for a nearby source of supply that gives prompt delivery too. The supplier may be asked to carry the inventory. Sometimes one may charge for transportation. But this arrangement will sale lot of money tied up in long-term inventory.

When suppliers offer quantity discounts one must see that the savings is not offset by other costs. One can negotiate a year's supply in order to get quantity discounts, then demand that the goods be supplied in small quantities as and when one needs them.

One can look for faster quick and cheaper transportation modes. It is better to keep the inventory only as finished goods. One can expand the concept of time. If it takes six weeks for delivery one does not need a six-week supply, as one can order smaller quantities for weekly or daily delivery.

The businessmen have to shop round for best price and group purchase are suggested. In case a rented warehouse is established by the supplier one can prefer such a supplier.

Other Suggestions for Improvement

It has been found that large scale industries dominate the market and they do not allow the small industries to come up. Purchase of raw materials can be made on co-operative basis. Regulated markets functioning in the districts can also render services of this nature.

The civil supplies corporation can establish warehouses to preserve groundnut at a very meagre rate of Rent to the agricultural farmers. Revolving credit facility system could be followed in this connection and commercial banks can give guarantee to the suppliers who extend revolving credit system. Electricity can be supplied at a concessional rate. Subsidy may be granted to the cultivators which may reduce the cost of production in total.

The Government can allot more funds towards Research and Developments in the field of agriculture in general and commercial oil seed crops in particular. Western pattern of production (cultivation) could be introduced by the Department of Agriculture in every district by selecting unemployed graduates who have atleast little property for cultivation. Co-operative farming to a certain extend can also be thought of with the help of establishing cooperative societies in the regard. Training the graduates can be imparted at a low cost quickly.

The idle decorticating machines available in the co-operative societies can be made good by the Government of Tamil Nadu which will be of much benefit to the poor entrepreneurs.

The impace, on implementation of the above said suggestion may be that, there will be more employment generation, more benefit to the agriculturists and entrepreneurs, and more income to the nation. This may also prove that the rural area itself will get developed economically and socially.

REFERENCES

1. Agarwal.A.N., *Indian Economy, Problems of Development & Planning*, 21st edition-Wishwa Prakashan, 1995.
2. *Entrepreneurship Development*, Centre for Research & Industrial Staff Performance, Bhopal. TATA McGraw-Hill Publishing Co. Ltd., New Delhi.
3. Memoria, CB & Tripathi B.B., *Agricultural Problems of India*, Kitab Mahal, Allahabad, 1997.
4. *District Profile*, Department of Statistics, Theni District.
5. Small Industries Development Organisation & Eigth Five Year Plan 1992-97 and 1998-99.
6. State Directories of Industries, Govt. of Tamil Nadu, Chennai.

20

Entrepreneurs in Rural Industries

Problems and Prospects

E. ANAND AND N. MEENAKSHISUNDARAM

In India about 73 per cent of people are living in the rural areas. Though the rural people are facing a number of problems in their life, getting adequate food and suitable accommodation are the major issue. To overcome the above problem appropriate technology in habitat played a wider role in building their life. The small entrepreneurs of the rural and urban area can be engaged in the production and marketing consumable goods which can be produced with lesser capital. There are many more cottage and small-scale industries, which are suitable to small entrepreneurs such as bakery, detergent powder, detergent cake, liquid blue and shampoo etc. These industries are capital cheap and labour intensive since all these goods are consumable items, which are required for our day-to-day life, they can be easily marketed in the local area.

The Role of Entrepreneurs

Employment

Entrepreneurs not only self employed but also provide employment to others. So they play an important role in helping the government in reducing unemployment problem.

Optimization of Capital

Small-scale firms require less capital per unit of out put and provide quick returns on investment due to shorter gestation period. In a capital scarce economy like India, small-scale sector can become a stabilizing force by providing high output capital ratio as well as rural employment.

Balanced Regional Development

Small scale industries in rural areas established by rural entrepreneur help to remove regional disparities by industrializing rural and backward areas. They also reduce the problems of congestion, slums and pollution in cities providing employment and income in rural areas and help in improving the living in those areas.

Mobilization of Local Resources

These entrepreneurs help to mobilize and utilize the local resources like small savings entrepreneur talent, which might otherwise remain idle or unutilized. They help to perfect and promote traditional family skills and handcrafts.

Foreign Exchange

Small – scale industries particularly in rural areas help in reducing pressure on the country's balance of payment in two ways. First, they do not require imports of sophisticated machinery or new materials secondly; these industries earn valuable foreign exchange through exports.

Consumer Surplus

Entrepreneurs in their rural industries produce a wide range of mass consumption items. Over 5000 products are being manufactured and providing goods of daily usage on a large scale small industries play a complementary role to large sectors. They provide parts, components and accessories to large-scale industries.

The following are some of the rural industries suitable for entrepreneurs:

1 Ghani Oil Industry

Edible oil is a part of our day-to-day food items and there is great demand for edible oil in India. Human diet essentially consists of proteins, carbohydrates, fats, salts, minerals and vitamins. The first three accounts for a large portion and fat have other functions also to perform. The function of carbohydrate is to burn up in the body and liberate energy, which is so essential for muscular activity.

The annual production of edible seeds in our country was 220 lakhs tons in 2001-2002. The country has produced 72 lakhs tons of edible oil with the above oil seeds. The demand for edible oil was far higher and considerable quantities of edible oil was imported by the country during last year.

As per the latest figures available there are 3 lakhs ghanis existing in our country with a total crushing capacity of 30 lakh tons of oil seeds, annually. It is also estimated that in our country the factory sector consisting of rotaries, expellers, salvent plants are having an annual crushing capacity of 150 lakh tons. Out of this, the salvent extraction plants alone numbering 181, have a crushing capacity of 44 lakh tons. According to one rough estimate, out of the total availability of oil seeds in our country the ghanis are able to get about 15 to 18 lakh for crushing and the rest in crushed in mills.

(1) Raw materials: Edible oil seeds (locally available).
(2) The capital requirement for the above industry will be Rs. 60,000.

2. Agarbathi Industry

Burning of Bathis (Udubathis) in religions and social functions is a practice in India. This industry capital investment is very low. Simple technology is used for production. The products should be produced and marketed at the villages. Therefore, the entrepreneur may start this business :

(1) Raw materials: charcoal powder, sandal wood powder, Gigathu, Marikolundu powder, Aromatics and other Perfumes.

3. Cleaning Powder

The cleaning powder is mainly used to clean the household utensils, enamel vessels etc. The capital investment for this industry is very low. Production period is very short. This industry mainly used locally available raw material and manpower. There is a very good market demand for this product. Therefore, the entrepreneur can make high profit in this business :

(1) Raw materials: Calcite powder, soda ash, Acid slurry, sodium meta silicate, Trisodium phosphate etc.
(2) Total capital required for this industry is Rs. 50, 000.

4. Honey Processing

Honey is the nature's gift, which has got high market demand. Therefore the entrepreneur can make high profit in this business :

(1) Raw materials: Raw honey
(2) Total capital required for this industry will be Rs. 1,00,000.

5. Bakery

Bakery products are a part of our day-to-day food. There is a good market demand for this product. Bakery industry is said to be a profitable industry. The rate of profit earned by bakery is based on the type of products manufactured by it. Bun, bread, rusk, vargis may not earn much profit. Most of the small bakeries have to manufacture the above items though the rate of profit is low, as there is demand in the rural areas. On the other hand stall bakers, who are having sales show room in the urban and sub-urban areas produce, cakes, puffs, cookies etc., and earn more profit. These products will fetch more profit though there is less sales. The stall bakers may also produce bun, bread, vargis etc., at low quantity. In order to have a combination of products or product mix to maximize the profit in bakery industry :

(1) Raw material: Maida, Sugar, Yeast, Salt, Water, Egg, Foreword/Fuel and fat.
(2) Total capital required for this industry is Rs. 30,000.

6. Paper Bag and Cup

Paper cup is such a commodity, which now a day plays an indispensable role in our life. The large public gathering, Get – together, tea – party, marriage, official meetings, seminars etc, the conventional glass, metal and porcelain containers have been utilized for offering beverages, tea, coffee, drinking water, fresh juices and other home made liquid drinks in the recent past sine acquiring and maintaining these conventional containers are expensive and often unhygienic, the plastic cups have been found as a suitable alternate.

The polythin bags are playing major role in packing and packaging purpose all the goods are now packing in the polythin bags. But polythene bags are thrown on the street it makes very worst environmental problems. This plastic bags are not bio-degradable. It takes more than 100 years to decompose, at the same time it is not good for earth. It pollutes the earth now the government passes the law to the eye of polythene bags there is no alternative for this polythin bags. But only the paper bag is the only suitable alternative for polythin bags. Therefore the entrepreneur can make high profit in this business. So the government encourage the entrepreneur to start paper bag units.

(1) Raw materials: Scoring and punching, cycling machine, paper cutting machine and accessories.
(2) Total capital required for this industry is Rs. 1,00,000.

7. Detergent Cake

The detergent cake is mainly used to clean the cloth. There is vast scope for this industry to Entrepreneur. These products fetch more profit though there is less sales. So the government encourage the entrepreneur to start detergent cake unit :

(1) Raw materials: Stone powder, soda ash, china clay, STPP, TSP, Acid Slurry, Sodium silicate, Starch, Perfume and colour.
(2) The capital requirement for can above industry will be Rs. 1,00,000/-.

8. Detergent Powder

Washing cloth is necessary to remove dirt. So, there is a very good market demand for this product. The capital investment for this industry is very less. Therefore, the entrepreneur can make high profit in this business.

(1) Raw materials: Washing soda, sodium sulphate, dalumide, colour, salt, perfume, water, caustic lye, acid slurry.

(2) Total capital required for this industry is Rs. 50,000.

9. Black phenyle

The black phenyle is mainly used to clean bathroom and toilets :

(1) Raw materials: Rosin, castor oil, cresote oil, caustic soda solution and water.
(2) Total capital required for this industry is Rs. 25,000.

10. Computer Aided Textile Design Unit

Designing cloth is very important element for increase production and sales operations. The design art work is essential to create figure suitable for particular portion of the fabric, or otherwise, the design already available is done on the computer by scanning. The scanned figure may be altered or resize according to the requirement.

Whenever input dates like size of the design, count of thread, ends per inch, picks per inch, warp and weft colour, weave specification to different colours for the design and art work, the actual design is simulated on VDU (Visual Display Unit) :

(1) Raw materials: Monitor, CPU, Key board, Mouse, Dot matrix, Printer, Scanner, UPS and software.
(2) Total capital required for this unit is Rs. 50,000.

There is vast scope for entrepreneurs in food preservation, bakery, handmade paper, dairy, poultry, hand loom, handicrafts and gem cutting etc. The Government and the NGO's in the development of entrepreneures in rural areas with the ultimate goal of bringing prosperity to entrepreneurs.

Problems Faced by Rural Entrepreneurs

The rapid growth of rural sectors has been marked by some problems such as technological stagnation, under utilization of capacity, lack of vertical mobility, sickness and high mortality rate. Small-scale industries in India face several practical problems and constraints, some of the problems are given below.

Shortage of Finance

Due to limited assets and low good will entrepreneurs often find it difficult to meet their fixed and working capital needs. Very few can avoil the single window scheme of the Small Industries Development bank of India. Entrepreneurs do not have property in their name/owing to the lack of confidence in male members for running business.

Shortage of Raw materials

The problem of raw materials is intimately related to lack of adequate working capital. Some times, the raw materials are available but the entrepreneurs do not have the working capital to procure them. In other cases, small scale units do not get the required raw materials in time for their product plans and delivery schedules. Some scarce raw material are distributed by state agencies at controlled prices. These agencies do not have the required quantity of the raw materials their procedure of procurement and buffer stocking are inappropriate and distortions in distribution add to the problem.

Inadequate Marketing Facilities

Due to their small size, small-scale industries are not in a position to market their product outside their regional locations. They find it very difficult to get remunerative prices due to their poor distribution network, insufficient advertising, middle man's exploitation and lack of uniform quality.

Outdated Technology

Most of the small-scale units cannot afford to employ latest machinery or equipment due to resource constraint. They don't undertake regular research and development to upgrade their process and technologies. In the absence of modern technology the productivity and quality suffer and cost of production tends to be high.

Lack of Trained Personnel

New entrepreneurs often suffer due to lack of experience and expertise in technical matters or in management. Established entrepreneurs do not have to access the latest information. Small – scale entrepreneurs do not interact regularly with the sources of knowledge and information.

Inadequate Infrastructure

Insufficient quantity and quality of industrial infrastructure particularly in the less developed regions in the other problem faced by the rural entrepreneurs. Infrastructure gap results in under utilization of the capacity and wastages.

Stiff Competition

Many of the entrepreneurs have poor organizational setup. They have to face severe competition from organized industries and particularly women with the male entrepreneurs.

Low Mobility

One of the biggest handicap for rural entrepreneurs is mobility in travelling from place to place. Women on their own find it difficult to get accommodation in smaller towns.

Prospects of Rural Entrepreneurs

The Government have established all India boards such as KVIC, Coir board, Silk board, Handloom board etc., several Non–Government social organization are also coming forward to train and support the rural entrepreneurs in teaching the skills, financing, project training and several other aspects.

Government is supporting the rural entrepreneurs by providing the training and supplying raw materials, implication of laws, rules, procedures, cluster approach, reservation policy, Establishment of Industrial co-operative, improvement in production methods and implements, producing goods of superior quality and new designs, provision for industrial education and training, improvement in marketing and raising competitive strength. The above prospects are required for the rural entrepreneurs.

Policy Recommendations to Solve the Problems of Rural Entrepreneurs

The following measures can be adopted to solve their problems.

Finance Cells

In various public financial institutions and banks special cells may be opened for providing easy finance to rural entrepreneurs. Efforts should be made to provide the finance at the local level. Finance should be provided at concessional rates of interest.

Marketing Co-operatives

Encouragement and assistance should be provided for setting up co-operatives. These co-operatives will pool the input of rural entrepreneurs and sell them on remunerative prices. Such co-operatives will help to eliminate the middlemen central and state governments should give priority particularly to these entrepreneurs while purchasing their requirements.

Supply of Raw Materials

Scarce and imported raw materials may be made available to these entrepreneurs on priority basis. A subsidy may be also be given to make the products manufactured by them cost competitive.

Education and Awareness

It is necessary to change negative social attitudes towards women particularly. Elderly members in the family such as mother, mother in law, need to be more aware of the potential of girls and their due role in society unless the social attitudes are made positive not much progress can be made.

Training Facilities

Training schemes must be designed to train particularly the rural small entrepreneurs must gain full advantage of these. As small entrepreneurs are not allowed to go far away for training by their family members, mobile training centres must be arranged.

Conclusion

To sum up the entire analysis in this article, it is observed that rural small entrepreneur in particular need to examine their inner potential and resistances. Hence extra support from within and out side source are is needed for rural entrepreneurs. The rural entrepreneurs constitute a significant segment in the Indian population and till now they have not been the focus to entrepreneurial development.

REFERENCES

1. Saravanavel, S., *Entrepreneurs Development*, New Delhi, 1999.
2. Pareek, V., *Development of Entrepreneurship A conceptional Model Developing Entrepreneurship Learning Systems*, New Delhi, 1998.
3. Srivastava, S.B., *A Practical Guide to Industrial Entrepreneurs*, 1998.
4. Wayne, G.B., *The Village Entrepreneur*, Harward University, Press, England, 1978.
5. Navendra Kumar, *Women Entrepreneurship Development in India, Problem and Prospects*, Indian Institute of Public Opinion, 1997.

21

Role of Rural Industrialisation in Sustainable Indian Agriculture

A. MOHAMED JAFFAR AND G. GANESAN

Introduction

Agriculture development is the prerequisite for the economic development of third world countries. Agriculture is an industry or business employing knowledge of the various sciences for the production of food, feed, fibre and fuel. India has made a lot of progress in agriculture since independence in terms of growth in output, yields and area under many crops. It has gone through a green revolution, white revolution, yellow revolution, blue revolution and now the 'rainbow revolution'. Today, India is the largest producer of milk, fruits, cashew nuts, coconuts and tea in the world, the second largest producer of wheat, vegetables, sugar and fish and the third largest producer of tobacco and rice.

Table 21.1 : Share of Export of Agricultural Products in Total Exports (Rs. Crore)

Year	*Total Exports*	*Agricultural Exports*	*% share*
1992-93	53,688	7,884	14.7
1993-94	69,751	13,021	18.7
1994-95	82,674	13,710	16.6
1995-96	1,06,353	21,136	19.8
1996-97	1,18,817	24,241	20.4
1997-98	1,26,290	23,690	18.8

Source : Indian Agriculture, Vikas Singhal, IEDRC, New Delhi, 1999, p.4.

Indian agriculture sector accounts for 28 per cent of its GDP and almost 75 per cent of India's population is rural based and attached to agriculture sector. But the market share of agriculture is projected to drop to 10.6 per cent in 2005.

The Central Govt. has announced the new National Agriculture Policy envisaging more than 4 per cent annual growth rate. A major highlight of the new policy is promotion of Private Sector participation through contract farming and land leasing arrangements to allow accelerated technology transfer, capital inflow and assured markets for crop production, especially of oil seeds, cotton and horticultural crops. Lease markets will be developed for increasing the size of holdings, and legal provisions will be made for giving Private Land on lease for cultivation and agro-business. It aims to achieve sustainable development of agriculture, create gainful employment on a self-sustaining basis in rural areas and raise the farmers' standards of living.

In the 2001-02 budget also Government announced much favourable terms to speed up the agricultural sector reforms and rural development. More investments declared in the improvement of infrastructure like rural roads and rural electrification.

The issue of providing more employment opportunities to the rural poor has become a matter of priority. Unemployment and underemployment are the chronic economic diseases in India. About 58 per cent of rural population are living below poverty line without any gainful employment even for a minimum of 90 days in a year. The employment growth rate has recorded a considerable decline from 2.8 per cent in 1972-73 to 1.41 per cent in 1991-92. According to an estimate the number of people looking for jobs has crossed 65 million persons by 1992-93 and about 62 per cent of it can be identified in rural area.

Many of the industrial units in India have been concentrated around a few metropolitan cities and urban towns. To avoid regional imbalance in India, development of entrepreneurship in backward regions has been adopted as a basic strategy of economic planning. Entrepreneurs can setup industries in backward areas to avail various concessions and subsidies offered by the central and state governments.

At village level there are a number of enterprises, which can given huge profits to the investors, more employment to youth and accelerate agricultural development in India.

Viable Agro Industries

(1) Crop Production

It is based on the land holdings. Growing of high yielding paddy of late duration variety is profitable. Similarly groundnut is a very profitable crop. The Sugarcane cultivation now gaining popularity and is quite remunerative as both supply of inputs and marketing is ensured by the sugar mills functioning in the area.

(2) Vegetable Farming

Vegetable farming is a boon for small and marginal farmers. Growing of off-season vegetable is more profitable. These are the reasons for which youths are inclined for vegetable farming. In Tamil Nadu, Uzhavar Santhai (Farmer Market) is serving honestly as middlemen in marketing the vegetables of the farmers.

(3) Mushroom Cultivation

Mushroom cultivation is becoming popular among village women. The raw materials like straw is abundantly available. There is demand for this product. It is mostly consumed by upper class people of the society. This product can gain popularity among middle and lower class people.

(4) Raising of Seedlings

Raising of seedlings of different crops and selling them at higher rate has become a practice in the urban areas. Raising of seedlings in the rural area is very profitable. By application of recommended practices, sound, healthy and disease free seedlings can be raised to meet the requirements of neighbouring farmers.

(5) Dairy

India is the third largest milk producer with its annual milk production at around 56 million tonnes. Of this, about 30 per cent is being converted into milk products with ghee alone accounting for more than 85 per cent. Development of the milk product industry is, however, dependent on the availability of liquid milk in adequate quantity and increase in milk output per cattle. It is an enterprise for earning of livelihood. It is established that a youth keeping three to four cows can comfortably earn to meet his family requirements. This enterprise can provide employment throughout the year but one has to plan carefully dairy farming, keeping continuous milking period in view.

(6) Livestock Products

India has the largest cattle population in the wold with the potential to be one of the top producers of meat and meat products. Sheep are reared for wool and goats for both milk and meat. Only pigs and poultry are reared for meat purposes. Poultry farming both for layers and table purpose is profitable. In many villages, people are acquainted with poultry keeping. To make poultry a means of living, many take this enterprise for the reason of heavy market demand and high price of goat-meat in the locality. For large scale sheep, goat or poultry farming bank credit is a must.

(7) Fish Products

India has vast potential for fishes from both in land and marine resources. With a coast line of 7,500 kms and an Exclusive Economic Zone (EEZ) of 2.02 million sq km the country is expected to have a potential of 4.0 million MT of marine fish production. The fish is in demand in the locality. The cost of production is much less compared to profit. Suitable area can be identified for the development of inland and coastal acquaculture. The fishery resources of India are said to be grossly under-utilized with tremendous potential to increase the output in the sector.

(8) Sericulture

Sericulture is an important labour intensive and agro based cottage industry providing employment to about 59 lakh persons in the rural and semi-urban areas in India. Of these, a sizeable number of workers belong to the economically weaker sections of the society. For women especially, this industry offers ample scope for profitable self-employment.

In the production of raw silk, India holds the second position in the world next to China. The Central Silk Board is the statutory organisation responsible for the implementation of developmental schemes in sericulture. To provide technical manpower for sericulture an International Centre for Training and Research in Tropical

Sericulture (ICTRETS) has been setup in Mysore. The centre offers diploma courses in tropical sericulture and sericulture management.

(9) Handloom Industry

The handloom industry provides the largest employment among the traditional industries, next to agriculture. The production of handloom cloth in 1993-94 is estimated at 5440 million sq. meters. In 1993-94, the handloom sector provided employment to 110 lakh persons. The Ministry of Textiles has formulated a package of schemes to promote handloom sector under IRDP, TRYSEM, IAY, etc., in consultation with the Ministry of Rural Development.

(10) Handicrafts

Handicrafts occupy an important position in the economy of the country both from the point of view of its employment and export potential. The employment in the handicrafts sector has increased from 35.8 lakh persons in 1989-90 to 53.1 lakh persons in 1992-93. The production has also increased from Rs.11,325 crores in 1990-91 to Rs.18,482 crores in 1993-94.

The Office of the Development Commissioner (Handicrafts) is the principal agency for the implementation of schemes aimed at the promotion of the handicrafts sector. To serve this dispersed sector having a wide range of products, the concept of crafts development centres in identified crafts pockets has been adopted.

(11) Coir Industry

The coir industry provides employment to about 5.5 lakh persons which is mostly part-time in nature. The industry offers substantial employment opportunities for women artisans. Coconut husk is the base raw material for coir products. Presently only around 50 per cent of the available coir husk is used to produce coir products. There is scope for further growth of coir industry. The total production of coir fibre has been estimated at 2.29 lakh tonnes in 1992-93. The Coir Board of India is the nodal agency for the implementation of promotional schemes for the coir industry. Two major institutes, the Central Coir Research Institute, Kerala and the Central Institute of Coir Technology, Bangalore, are carrying out R & D programmes in areas of improvement in productivity and reduction in drudgery of coir workers.

(12) Consumer Food Industries

Packaged food products coming under this sub-sector comprise mainly of the following products: (i) Bread, biscuits and other bakery products, (ii) Confectionery, chocolates and cocoa products, (iii) Soft drinks, iv) Semi-processed and ready to eat (RTE) foods. In the area of bread and related products more than 90 per cent of the units are in the cottage sector with the units decentralized and spread throughout the country. The soft drinks sector covers non-alcoholic flavoured beverages. The size of the Indian semi-processed and RTE foods industry is estimated at over Rs.40 billion, with the market for these products estimated to be growing at over 20 per cent.

(13) Primary Food Processing

Primary food processing, includes grain processing and pulse milling. Grain processing includes rice milling, flour milling and pulses. Processing is the biggest component in the food sector constituting over 70 per cent of the total value added. Flour milling in the organized sector is done through licensed flour mills. Pulse milling is also mostly in the unorganized sector. About 10-15 per cent of the pulses are lost due to the obsolete technology adopted. There is thus considerable scope for the modernization of production and processing methods.

(14) Floriculture

According to an estimate the area under floricultural crops in India is about 60,000 ha, of which 40,000ha are under traditional flowers like jasmine, marigold, crossandra, rose, chrysanthemum, aster, tuber rose, etc., and 20,000 ha under contemporary cut flower crops like rose, Chrysanthemum, Carnation, gladiolus, tuber rose, gerbera, orchid lilies, etc. The important flower growing states in India are Karnataka, Tamil Nadu, Maharashtra, West Bengal, Andhra Pradesh and Rajasthan. In India, the area under jasmine is about 10,000 ha and the production is worth Rs.80-100 million annually. The export of floriculture products from India has gone up from 7.8 crores in 1990-91 to 57.8 crores in 1995-96. India has a very small share in the global trade of $6 billion to 7 billion of cut flowers and potted plants. India's major buyers are UK, Germany, Netherlands and Switzerland. Floriculture is one sector where India has very good opportunities to boost up exports. The floricultural industry has annual growth potential of 25 per cent to 30 per cent.

Role of the Government

Indian Government is taking much efforts to develop rural industries. The operation of the Rural Infrastructure Development Fund (RIDF), set up in 1995-96 with NABARD, has been successful in upgrading rural infrastructure with about 1,84,000 projects sanctioned so far. The present budget (2001-02) reduced the interest rate charged by NABARD from 11.5 per cent to 10.5 per cent and assured, in next year the Corpus of RIDF VII will be increased from Rs.4,500 crores to 5,000 crores. Food processing industry dealing in Perishable fruits and vegetables is completely exempted from excise duty of this budget. This will include a very wide range of products of common use like Pickles, Sauces, Ketchup and Juices, etc.

Conclusion

In the rural area, government agencies and financial institutions like venture capital funds should come forward to uplift agro based industries by way of providing financial assistance, infrastructure facilities and vital training and development on entrepreneurship. These funding agencies can enjoy the profits as value added benefits of Agro industries.

Thus, the rural industrialization will be the basis for sustainable agriculture in India.

REFERENCES

1. Amarendra, *Poverty, Rural Development and Public Policy*, Deep & Deep Publications, 1998.
2. Datt and Sundaram, *Indian Economy*, S.Chand & Co., 2000.
3. Kinsely, B.H., *Agri business and Rural Enterprise*. Croom Helm, London, 1987.
4. Krishna Rao, B., *Development Policy – A Study of Indian Perspective*, Sterling Publishers, 1993.
5. Vikas Singhal, *Indian Agriculture*, IEDRC, New Delhi, 1999.
6. Vishnu Swarup, *Ornamental Horticulture*, Macmillan India Ltd., 1997.

The Contributors

Anand, E.
Department of Rural Industries and Management,
Gandhigram Rural Institute,
Gandhigram.

Arumukham, P.
Former Professor & Head,
Department of Rural Development,
Gandhigram Rural Institute,
Gandhigram.

Ayyadurai, K.
Reader in Commerce,
Arulanandar College,
Karumathur,
Madurai.

Balasubramani, K.
Department of Rural Industries and Management,
Gandhigram Rural Institute,
Gandhigram.

Ganesan, S.
Director Incharge,
Alagappa Institute of Management,
Alagappa University,
Karaikudi, Tamil Nadu.

Ganesan, G.
Lecturer in Commerce, Periyar Arts College,
Kadalur.

Gopalsamy, V.
PSR Engineering college,
Kovilpatti.

Kanniappan, P.
Registrar, Gandhigram Rural Institute,
Gandhigram.

Mariajohn, S.
Reader in Commerce,
C.P.A. College,
Bodi.

Mathew, Oommen
Professor,
Institute of Management in Government,
Cochin, Kerala.

Meena, K.
Principle and Head,
Dept. of Computer Science,
Shrimati Indra Gandhi College,
Prichy, Tamil Nadu.

Meenakshisundaram, N.
Professor,
Department of Rural Industries and Management,
Gandhigram Rural Institute,
Gandhigram. Dindigul District. Tamil Nadu.

Muhammed Jafar, A.
Reader in Commerce, H.K.R.H. College,
Uthamapalayam.

Murugesan, K.
Seminar Technical Assistant,
Department of Rural Industries and Management,
Gandhigram Rural Institute,
Gandhigram.

Radhakrishnan, S.
Department of Rural Industries and Management,
Gandhigram Rural Institute,
Gandhigram.

Raja *alias* Pranmalai, K.
Lecturer,
Department of Rural Industries and Management,
Gandhigram Rural Institute,
Gandhigram.

Ramaswamy, S.
Reader,
Department of Economics,
Gandhigram Rural Institute,
Gandhigram.

Ramesh Babu, S.
Management Consultant,
31, Kairali Apartment,
Panampilly Nagar,
Cochin, Kerala.

Rathakrishnan L.
Reader,
Department of Rural Industries and Management,
Gandhigram Rural Institute,
Gandhigram.

Sankaran, H.
Assistant General Manager – HRD,
Beacon Weir Limited,
Chennai-98.

Seerangarajan, R.
Reader in Khadi Handloom Technology,
Department of Rural Industries and Management,
Gandhigram Rural Institute,
Gandhigram.

Vaijayanthi, P.
Asst. Professor,
School of Management SASTRA Deemed University,
Tirumalaisamudram-Thanjavur, Tamil Nadu.

Index